# OLD BEAN'S LAST FANTASY

# SANDRA CHAIT

# OLD BEAN'S
# LAST
# FANTASY

## A LATE-LIFE COMING-OF-AGE STORY

*This is a work of fiction. Names, characters, and incidences are either the product of the author's imagination or are used fictitiously.*

OLD BEAN'S LAST FANTASY
*A Late-Life Coming-of-Age Story*

FIRST EDITION

ISBN    978-1-5445-4740-4   *Hardcover*
          978-1-5445-4739-8   *Paperback*
          978-1-5445-4738-1   *Ebook*

To my husband, Alan.

# CHAPTER 1

————

SHE COULD FEEL THE ELECTRICITY, LIKE A BUZZ IN THE Seattle air that hinted at possibilities. Although she didn't know what happened in the techie world of Microsoft, Amazon, and Google, their South Lake Union neighborhood felt to her as charged as an orchestra warming up before a performance. Throughout the area, startups, biotechs, and technology companies packed the city blocks, standing flush against one another as if proximity could impart osmosis. As she walked through the sparsely populated after-lunch streets, she imagined momentous ideas flaming, flaring, and fighting one another behind the companies' many-eyed buildings. The combustion of those ideas, she believed, emitted an electrifying energy that surged through her body and ignited her desire to be a part of it all.

At her age, of course, she knew she had no chance of being involved in the technical revolution that had subsumed Seattle. She would sometimes picture herself brainstorming with smart young men and women who welcomed her into their midst. Inspired by their youthful creativity, her brain would sprout wild and brilliant ideas that would make her giddy with adrenaline. A moment later, however, she would sense those ephemeral thoughts flutter to the ground and, like dying fish, lie there valiantly flicking their tail fins. No, she could never be part of the techies' creative ferment. She just happened to live in the same neighborhood, where she listened hungrily to the sounds of their exciting world passing her by.

Still, while she was no spring chicken, and her 75-year-old brain sometimes short-circuited, Roberta Glazer—Bertie, as her friends called her—did not suffer from ontological despair, nor did she have one foot in the grave.

Which is precisely what she told the concierge, Michael, as she wheeled her shopping basket into the lobby of Mariela Plaza, and through her headphones heard him ask, "Can I help you with those heavy groceries, Mrs. Glazer?" She could not deny that the basket felt heavy, what with the two bottles of sauvignon she'd included with her groceries, but she was perfectly capable of pulling her cart into the elevator, having already lugged it on and off the South Lake Union trolley. Normally, she even walked the entire way to and from Whole Foods, but the Seattle forecast had predicted rain and, though she had become one of those Seattleites who proudly challenged the sky umbrella-less, she preferred not to get drenched. As for Michael's offer, well…it was awfully nice of the solicitous young concierge to make her feel seen, especially after the supermarket cashier had bypassed her to slobber over the suave young man behind her in line. But then Michael was paid to be attentive to the apartment residents, wasn't he? No matter how old the residents were, that was his job. Besides, shouldn't he save his concern for people who needed it, like the perky old guy from apartment 2010, the louche lech with the red beret who whipped around in his wheelchair and winked at her whenever she passed him in the foyer? Sometimes she wondered whether she should be grateful for 2010's attention, whether she should take her winks wherever she could get them.

"So, how many pages have you put together since I last saw you?" She slipped the headphones down her neck like the techies she saw in their hood. It annoyed her that she had to interrupt Creedence Clearwater Revival (CCR), especially at her favorite cut "Who'll Stop The Rain," but the lobby clock read almost three, and she knew her bugging Michael about his thesis would cut short their interaction. He had been struggling with his PhD for the last four years and seemed no closer to finishing than when they had first crossed paths. He smiled sheepishly, doing that in-place, circular footwork that suggested he wanted to be anywhere but there.

"I plan to keep checking on you, young man," she said to his averted face. She hadn't seen him write a single word other than the odd equations he sometimes scribbled, like hieroglyphics, on the back of apartment flyers. When he held open the elevator door and pressed the twentieth-floor button for her, she said something encouraging, for he was a nice boy and she felt fond of him, but the door closed and soon she was zooming up the chute, watching the numbered lights ascend into the heavens.

Even as she did so, the voice of her Pilates teacher, Christin, played over and over in her head, like a stuck record. Not that the 20-year-old instructor would have any idea of a vinyl record or the irritating sound it made when the needle got stuck in a groove, but her endlessly chipper voice came to Bertie now reminding her of her pelvic-floor exercises. "Pretend you are standing in an elevator. As the elevator rises in the chute, imagine drawing your pelvic muscles up…and up…and up…"

Outside number 2045, having released her pelvic muscles from their routine, Bertie fumbled with her keys, then braced herself against the heavy fireproof door to wheel the cart through the opening before it slammed shut. Luckily, she was a woman of some heft, as people now say, though she'd heard worse from those inclined to more shaming words. Yet she wasn't fat in the sense of obese or flabby, just big and strong from years of swimming, running, and playing tennis. And then, too, there was all that heavy lifting of patients that in her young days had made her bodily strength as marketable as her nursing skills.

Once inside, her phone app switched on the kitchen lights, lifted the blinds, and set the kettle boiling. Given the building's position in techie land, the kitchens in Mariela Plaza boasted a plethora of high-tech gizmos. In the bathroom, a Toto toilet washed and air-dried her rear end, and in the study, where three different remotes frequently bamboozled her, she could change channels with her voice alone. If she had wished, a Roomba would have sped across the wooden floor, vacuuming dust invisible to her fading eyes. It was like another Michael from the lobby easing her life when all she really wanted was to remain self-reliant and independent. To tell the truth, she shouldn't even have been in such a fancy apartment—she and Lennie certainly couldn't afford it at the time—but their kids, having determined that their parents should spend their "last years" in a "comfortable place" requiring no upkeep, subsidized them. Kids, of course, knew what was best for their folks. Initially, a tad of orneriness on her part had made her resist the offer—after all, weren't she and Lennie capable of making their own decisions? But when the children's intentions so obviously arose from an honest place, she caved in, grateful that Alex and Arielle still cared that much for them.

From the framed picture on the entrance hall table, her dead Lennie greeted her with the same amused smile that had intrigued her in her twenties. It tugged at the corners of his mouth, creating a tiny indent on the left side like a cellulite dimple. As she lifted the supermarket bags from her cart in the kitchen, she reminded herself that come October, it would be two years since his death from Covid. Lennie had always been so energetic, so full of life, that nobody had expected him to succumb to the virus, least of all her. Now he was gone and with him, her sparring partner, her bedmate, and her rock.

But, enough of this nonsense, she scolded herself before she could fall back into that comforting, nostalgic trap and short-changing her memory. Ramming the wheeled basket against the wall in the corner, she reminded herself how often she had wanted to swipe that smug smile off Lennie's face, never sure if he nurtured an inside joke or an irony that he was not sharing with her.

She hadn't even finished unpacking the overpriced groceries in her state-of-the-art kitchen, when she heard the key turn in the front door, as it did every weekday afternoon at 3:00 p.m.

"Hi, Gran, did you get my favorite passion-fruit yogurt?" Lisa breezed in, touching two fingers to her grandpa's portrait, then bringing them to her lips in a ritual she had started when barely eleven, soon after Lennie's death. She and Lennie had spent only five years of her life living in the same place, but during that time, they had forged a tight bond and created a team tough enough to successfully negotiate bedtimes, clothes, and books.

"You are not helping!" Lisa's mom, Arielle, would frequently reprimand Lennie when he supported his granddaughter's side. "And wipe that mischievous smile off your face, Dad," when he and Lisa went off chuckling at their successful maneuvering.

She watched her granddaughter dump her bulky, sticker-covered backpack that screamed "Imagine world peas!" on the cream-colored sofa in the living room. Her old ballpoint stains already festooned one of the cushions, and she now added to the sofa's advancing pied pattern something dusty that hung from the backpack's strap. Soil? Better not to know. Back in the kitchen, Lisa rummaged through the rest of the packages until she found her favorite foodstuffs: almond butter and raisin-cinnamon bagels. Both scored high in calories but added not an ounce to her slim frame. On the fridge, her own smiling face photographed at different ages grinned back at her from the past, crowding out her scowling diva, asserting herself at two.

"Watch your fingers, sweetheart!" Bertie grimaced as her granddaughter sliced through the middle of the bagel with the bread knife, holding her fingers just slightly beyond the reach of the blade. When her mom was still a child, Bertie had encouraged Arielle to try out new skills, even dangerous ones like boiling water for tea, yet with Lisa…she didn't know…she had become quite the nag, always anxious that something dreadful might befall her granddaughter on her watch.

The girl appeared oblivious of any danger and having toasted and then smeared the bagel stood leaning against the counter licking the melted butter from her fingers. In her short tartan skirt and workman's boots with thick rolled socks, she looked simultaneously tough and vulnerable. Sometimes, on their walks to Jake's Deli round the corner to buy salami sandwiches, or to Pike Street Market for Friday-night flowers, Bertie noticed how men surreptitiously ogled the 13-year-old. Whether Lisa spotted them too, she didn't know, though she suspected that Lisa would have missed that thing their eyes were doing, "the male gaze" at that point being simply an abstraction she had learned about in school. Or so a grandmother liked to think. On the other hand, maybe it was her granddaughter's teetering on the cusp of womanhood that had persuaded Arielle to continue having Lisa come to Bertie's apartment after school, rather than go home to their empty house.

On a couple occasions when Bertie hadn't been available, Lisa had hung out among the young techies at her dad Alex's office at Sarssein, but since her twelfth-year growth spurt, he had nixed that. For Bertie, sharing her afternoons with her granddaughter proved the gift that kept giving. She counted herself lucky. Soon enough, she feared, Lisa would no longer need or even want her.

Bertie's watch pinged. A quick glance at the screen, which held a picture of baby-toothed Lisa as a 4-year-old mischief-maker, told her that Michael had a delivery for her downstairs, the books she'd preordered for family and friends as Hanukkah/Christmas presents. Buying from Amazon would have made her life easier and less expensive but…"Hell, no," Lisa informed her when she discovered her grandmother even considering it, "supporting that mammoth would perpetuate its hegemony." Having just acquired the word at school, she practiced using it on her grandmother—not always correctly. Each addition to Lisa's vocabulary evolved her thinking so that Bertie had to remind herself of the child's youth and not talk to her like she did with her best friends Marion and Daru, the other two not-quite Golden Girls of their Mariela Plaza triad.

A splattered blob of passion-fruit yogurt stuck to Lisa's dark curly hair where it had fallen loose from her scrunchie in a ringlet. At least she hadn't dyed her hair blue like some of her classmates, nor gone goth with black eyes and nose rings, though she wore the small ear studs Bertie gave her for her thirteenth birthday. Their color, teal like the Glassy Baby tumblers Seattleites loved, hinted at hidden levels and depths, like her eyes. Her mother's eyes too.

"So, how was your nemesis today?" she asked, wiping the yogurt off Lisa's hair, then running the blob from her finger under the swan-necked faucet that always sprayed when you wanted spurt. "Did you have any more trouble with him?"

"To think I actually felt sorry for him last week!" her granddaughter groaned between spoonsful of the creamy stuff. "He kept getting into trouble and, to be fair, teachers blame him for everything, even when he's not the culprit."

"But this week?"

"That's just it. This morning, to completely slay any sympathy I might have had, he demanded my math homework again."

"Couldn't you refuse?"

"No way! He just pinned me against the wall with his arms on either side of my head."

"And nobody said anything?" She tried not to let her concern show.

Any bright young man should have been terrified of making such a move lest the girl report him and trash his clean record. Despite articles about unwanted attention landing cocky young lads in trouble, it was obvious not all boys knew to ask permission before touching. While Bertie entertained reservations about certain #MeToo's excesses, if fear of it protected her granddaughter, she would not complain. In any case, as Lisa now told her, none of the girls in her class were likely to challenge the bully because they already drooled over him and would happily change places with her. He was dripping with rizz, they said.

"Charisma?" Bertie took a stab at the meaning.

"As for the boys..." She threw up her hands. "You would think Jared was some god, the way they follow him. Who knows why. Maybe because...because...I don't know, he's just so confident. He always gets what he wants."

She took a bite from her bagel and chewed vigorously before squirreling it in one cheek to repeat his words, informing her she had no rights, being his junior, and this was just the way of the world; that they might be in the same class, but he had two years on her, so there was nothing she could do about it.

"Balderdash!"

"Is that another of your old-fashioned words, Gran? Like 'tommyrot' and 'lollygagging'? It's ridiculous to use words from *your* day when nobody understands what you're talking about."

The words were from her father's day, but she still liked the sound of them. Where do such words go to die, she wondered, visualizing acres of word cemeteries disappearing into the distance, like falling dominoes. Even dictionaries eventually dropped them.

"Well, let me tell you one thing from 'my day' that may still apply," she suggested, wading into the teenage territory of her past. "When a boy bugged you, it usually meant he was trying to catch your attention. Maybe Jared just fancies you, and that was his way of..."

"Pu-u-leeze!" Lisa interrupted and stuck her finger down her throat.

No misunderstanding that gesture. So, Bertie offered her a cup of tea, another ritual she enjoyed, and the two of them sat on opposite sides of the kitchen table sipping their Lapsang souchong mixed with Earl Grey in the rose-petal China cups she insisted upon. They commiserated about bullies, and when Bertie recounted how Lisa's mother had once dealt with a mean school friend—Wendy—by branding her Windy and persuading her posse to do the same, she even elicited a giggle. Seeing that dimple so like Lennie's brightened her day. In school, where Lisa studied genetics, she gave thanks to the gods that had given her Lennie's nice dimple, but not his mole that had hairs growing out of it.

As Bertie sipped her tea, appreciating the interaction of the strong smoky flavor with the perfumed one, she could see from the way Lisa's teeth pulled down on her upper lip that she still struggled to make sense of what had happened with Jared.

"But why me?" she frowned, having rejected her grand-mother's suggestion of attraction. "He knows I'm not intimidated by him. Do you think there's something about me that..."

"No," Bertie forestalled her, "these things just happen, sweet-heart. Few people get through life without a bully or two, people who for one reason or another, want to get at you. We call them antagonists. Everyone must deal with them. Annoying though they are."

"Not you, surely? I mean, who would fight with an old woman?"

Bertie sipped her tea, then slowly replaced the cup in its saucer, wondering how best to answer without bad-mouthing anyone her granddaughter might know.

"Well, I do have an antagonist," she ventured, "but unlike yours, mine is inside of me. He's internal, so no one sees how he challenges me and pushes me to do things I shouldn't."

Lisa searched her face for some indication of terrible things her grandmother might have done, but perhaps her young mind could not imagine the mischief a 75-year-old could get into in the old days.

When Bertie explained no further, Lisa just shrugged her shoulders, and they moved on to her clarinet practice, plus the history and English homework, which was Bertie's grand-motherly duty to oversee. Lennie had never involved himself in teaching—nor cooking and disciplining, for that matter—because he just wanted to have fun, he always said. He wanted to play with his granddaughter, something he had done little of with his own daughter. Sometimes, when Lisa's eyes had lit up like a smart watch when her gramps entered the room, Bertie had felt envious. She knew Lisa loved her too, but she also took her for granted, a privilege of the young, she supposed. That was the thing about being old. You were just there, an entity to make others' lives easier, to allow others to have fun.

After Lennie's death, however, a strange thing happened. Fun slid unexpectedly through a side door during Covid, arriving in the unexpected form of online gaming. To Bertie, it initially seemed like just more of the child play that dominated her weekday life, edging her further and further away from the alluring adult concerns that roiled the creative world around her. But, as her learning progressed, gaming became an essential part of her and Lisa's weekday afternoons, bringing with it a sense of reckless fun and vicarious adventure, plus a shared intimacy she now considered inviolable.

Lisa plonked herself in front of Bertie's desktop. She had installed at least a dozen interactive games, which she had taught Bertie during the two years the virus had kept them all housebound. Although the rules of play seemed complicated to Bertie, Lisa had assured her they would become second nature after she had one or two under her belt, which had turned out to be so. Not that Bertie always relished shooting ogres or monsters, which characters dominated the whole game scene, but what? Was she going to refuse her teenage granddaughter, when she felt only gratitude that Lisa wanted to play with her? Even Dr. Meredith had encouraged Bertie, informing her that her reflexes needed honing, and sharpening them might also whet her brain.

Once she had the hang of how these games worked, the two of them went at it every weekday afternoon. Seated alongside each other at the console, hands and eyes moving swiftly as they took the measure of the land, they went in search of their goal, ready to butcher anything that got in their way. Joining them on screen, players from all over the world directed their avatars to leap and teleport just like theirs did to avoid the hazards the game threw in their paths.

In this afternoon's game, they committed to saving Arkesia with their gunlances and shields from the demons who threatened to destroy it. Many of the games they played, like *Lost Ark*, were graphically gorgeous and sometimes, in between the explosions and screams, the ethereal music would move Bertie with its beauty. She suspected that most young players didn't have time to appreciate either music or art, but she frequently stopped mid-action to admire one or the other, in the process getting obliterated by some hideous monstrosity with horns or a scorpion tail. Did graphic designers work in tandem with psychologists to find the most viscerally revolting entities? With a quick thrust of her lance, she demolished a familiar humpbacked monster who sometimes seeped from her dreams.

Eventually, exhausted from having to keep her wits about her, and with her head pounding like it had been bombarded from all sides, she left Lisa to it. She could play some other game solo while Bertie heated a snack that would tide her over until her dad picked her up to go home. Samosa, always a hit, topped her list of favorites. Occasionally, if Alex texted he would be late, Bertie would also cook the ginger, peanut, and tofu dishes that seemed to strike her granddaughter's taste buds just right. Chatting away in an easy camaraderie as they sliced and chopped at the kitchen table, they would barely notice time disappear until Alex called from the foyer to let them know he'd arrived.

From the living room, the shrill winging of bullets and the muffled sounds of explosions followed Bertie into the kitchen like a bad trip. Screams too. Not that screaming lay outside the ordinary sound effects of playing games that involved killing and being killed. Certain games simply elicited more verbal abuse than others. In any case, she had done her own share of shrieking when about to be eviscerated, or when she remembered something egregious the real Lennie (not the pedestaled one) had said or done. As she removed the samosa from the freezer, however, whatever game Lisa now played affronted her ears differently. Lisa's voice had leapfrogged an octave and Bertie's grandmotherly antennae shot up quivering.

"You fucker!" she heard, followed by the digital rat-a-tat-tat of an automatic weapon. "Suck on that, Jared, you jerk!" as she rained fire on some unsuspecting asteroid or meteor that had dared to thwart her wishes and was now transformed into her arch enemy, her number one.

As Bertie laid the Trader Joe's samosa on a microwave-safe plate, she wondered whether this afternoon's session had worsened Lisa's hearing. She really needed to talk to Arielle about it. The child should wear ear protection. The microwave beeped, and she gingerly slid out the plate, keeping it balanced so the samosa would not slide off. Now that Lisa had vanquished her antagonist and got Jared out of her system, she hoped she would hear no more of the loutish boy. Perhaps Lisa would even share her method of annihilation so Bertie could use it on her own humpbacked ghoul.

Engrossed in what she was doing, it took some time before Bertie noticed the deafening silence that now emanated from the other room. Gone now were the game's sound effects, the ephemeral music, and Lisa's angry verbiage. For a moment she wondered whether a sudden cyberattack had knocked out power in South Lake Union and left the area's techies marooned. Curious, she returned to the living room to find her granddaughter standing there as if in suspended animation, looking like a one-eyed bird readying itself for flight. Lisa wore a different headset now, one that resembled the underwater goggles of a cyborg. With her arms outstretched, she held in each hand a red plastic wheel that resembled the controllers they used in their online games.

"OMG! This is incredible, Gran! It's everywhere, all around me."

"What's incredible? What are you doing?" But Lisa didn't seem to hear a word. Bertie tugged at the sleeve of her T-shirt, and the cyborg turned reluctantly toward her, then removed the headset and laid it gently on Lennie's chair. It could have been a precious baby, so tenderly did Lisa set it down.

Then, turning to Bertie with a mischievous smile, her granddaughter put a finger to her lips. "Don't you dare tell Dad! He doesn't know I took it."

"Took what? What is it?" No wonder her backpack had looked bulgy today.

"It's Dad's new headset for stepping into 3D immersive VR. Can you believe it?"

Bertie couldn't. She had no idea what the child was talking about, nor could she believe Lisa had secretly pinched something from her dad's study. Shocked as she was about what Lisa had done, she knew, however, she would reveal nothing her granddaughter confided to her. Sometimes she wondered whether Alex and Arielle didn't perhaps leave Lisa in her care, hoping she would glean the girl's secrets and tell them. Fat chance! In any case, what could she tell them about this headset? She didn't even know what she was looking at. To Lisa, her face must have appeared confused and befuddled.

"See..." Lisa enlightened her, "ever since Facebook became Meta and started plowing money into the metaverse, Dad's been talking about nothing else. But I had no idea he was busy making his own version. Wow! All this time," she marveled, "and he's kept it a secret. He must have been working on it for months without me even knowing what he was up to. Still, a new headset to rival Oculus? I mean, Dad's business is just a gaming company! Sarssein is not like Meta or Microsoft."

She could barely contain her excitement, but Bertie still had little idea of what she was talking about. To her, the headset just looked like some white, plastic thing.

At seventy-five, being at a loss to understand the explanation of a 13-year-old disturbed Bertie, but it was happening more and more these days. Metaverse? Oculus? Immersive VR? These words mystified her. The world was changing before her eyes, and here she was, desperately grasping at its coattails.

"But why do all those companies want to step into 3D...what did you call it? Immersive VR?" she persisted, impatient to understand this recent development.

"To enter the metaverse, of course."

Her incredulity at her gran's ignorance made her dimple pulsate, reminding Bertie of Lennie.

"The metaverse? But sweetheart"—she took her granddaughter's hand—"what is it, this thing called the metaverse?"

The word hovered hesitantly between them: on Lisa's side referencing a world of infinite possibilities; on hers, signifying nothing.

# CHAPTER 2

———

THE MIST THAT SEATTLEITES CALL RAIN SPRITZED THE air. It sprayed fine particles of moisture onto the large glass windows of TechTown Café where Bertie sat waiting for her friend Marion Meisel. It also frizzed her hair and turned loose curls around her face into unflattering crinkles. The days of ironing her gray hair, of course, were long gone, but it still rankled her to look like a barbet or an Irish water spaniel, a resemblance that Marion first pointed out to her. "Affectionately," she'd said. Marion lived in the same apartment block and had been a good friend to both her and Lennie ever since they moved to Seattle from Vancouver. Bertie often hung out in Marion's apartment and Marion in hers, but every Wednesday morning, they made a point of meeting for coffee away from home.

Marion walked in now, stamping her feet and shaking her mane of dyed reddish hair though the mist had hardly touched it. She had been a litigation lawyer before she retired and still maintained something dramatic in her movements that made people look twice. Occasionally she even went out on dates, finding her victims in Mariela Plaza or through dating sites.

"Better than sitting alone in my apartment watching reruns of *The Golden Girls*," she'd countered when Bertie wondered aloud how she could put up with such old geezers.

"Hey." Bertie waved, and Marion came over and hugged her, dropping her commodious black bag on the table and sloshing Bertie's coffee. She had nurtured her favorite barista with big tips and some legal advice about his rent arrears so now she no longer needed to order at the counter like the rest of them. She simply caught Tom's eye and her double-shot latte in a real cup, not a paper one, arrived steaming in front of her.

"Hi, Marion. Hi, Roberta." Tom brushed Bertie's spilt sugar from the marble-topped table into his palm. "Anything else I can get you ladies?" He smiled, showing the perfectly white teeth of the fluoride generation. At 10:30 in the morning, he could afford to pay the women attention as the place had emptied like a beach after sundown. The rush of city employees inhaling their morning joe usually packed TechTown at 8:45, but by 9:00, everyone had disappeared. During Covid, with most techies working from home, it was Marion, Daru, Bertie, and a few locals who kept the place going and barista Tom employed.

Being called by their first names always pleased Bertie and Marion, as if it somehow reinserted them into the regular working world, making them visible again. Marion's ex had divorced her in her fifties when he fell for his lab assistant, who looked like a younger version of her, but though Marion had kept his surname for convenience, she felt little affinity for the sound of it. In those days, #MeToo hadn't been heard of and, if anyone wondered about the power disparity between boss and employee, nobody spoke up.

Through the overhead speakers, Brandi Carlile sang of throwing it all away, and Marion took the first few sips of her latte. After licking some froth from the corner of her mouth, she patted Bertie on the arm.

"So, Old Bean?" She addressed her, eye-to-eye, as she always did. You can get the woman out of New York, her ex used to say... In fact, Marion's directness often discomforted older people, especially Seattle's Scandinavian citizens unaccustomed to such intimate interaction. "Did that son-in-law of yours eventually get you and Lisa the ear protection you asked for?"

Though Bertie assured her Alex had indeed fixed the problem by resetting the volume on their game headsets to a safe decibel level, she went on and on about these techie types who concerned themselves with ones and zeros rather than people's comfort.

"Alex is not like that," Bertie assured her. "He adores Lisa and would never do anything to harm her. Look, I love Alex, but he's just a big child. He gets carried away when something technological excites him."

Together with a disgruntled philosophy graduate, Alex owned Sarssein, a gaming company that, despite conducting their work in stealth mode and steeping it in the utmost secrecy, had become known as one of the country's top players. In Sarssein's search for other being-in-the-world places, it developed fantasy games with Asian, Caribbean, or Middle Eastern bents. A good deal of its success, according to Arielle, derived from Alex's creativity and the way he enabled players to feel they could make it outside of their own small worlds. Bertie had seen some of Alex's work in the games Lisa had shown her, so she was inclined to believe Arielle despite her spousal bias. Thanks to Alex, Bertie possessed one of the most sophisticated PCs in Mariela Plaza with all kinds of bells and whistles, most of which functioned beyond her 75-year-old understanding.

"You have so much RAM, your computer bleats."

"Rams don't bleat," she grimaced at Marion, "they grumble."

Alex taught Lisa how to play the games Sarssein produced, and she, in turn, coached Bertie. To the kids in their neighborhood, if not their parents, Lisa's father was the candy man, the creator of all kinds of cool games. Some of Alex's technological gloss even wiped off on Bertie, leading the few children in their building to call her "that dope old woman"—a compliment, Lisa assured her, though she sometimes wondered about their intent. Kids today often used irony or said the opposite of what they meant.

By now, she was playing numerous games with Lisa besides those designed by her father. *Shadowlands*, *World of Warcraft*, and *Final Fantasy* were among her favorites, but also some dragon games, especially *Lost Ark*, though she had recently interacted with that solo because it gave her permission to let fly with all her petty grievances without Lisa seeing her erupt. She preferred too that her granddaughter didn't watch her scoop up baby dragon droppings. Sure, every gamer had to do it, just like picking up dog doo in real life, but part of her still wanted her granddaughter to perceive her as cool.

Lisa and she had been playing games the whole of last week and had started a new one that Alex had recently released. He hoped it would attract more young women and girls to the cause, but Lisa had nixed it as too wimpy and pastel by far. Add some heavy metal to the background, she'd suggested. Her father had listened and plans for a revised version of the game lay in the works. Such feedback from Lisa, she'd learnt, was not unusual. Sometimes, she even picked up on Bertie's comments and incorporated them into her critique.

"I don't know what's so appealing about those games."

Marion sat up straight, or as straight as you can in those curled, round chairs designed for youngsters.

"Isn't it all just violence and murder, and nonstop war... where winning means killing off your enemies and destroying everything that gets in your way? At least that is what I hear. Wouldn't play these things myself; such a waste of time. All that noise and chaos... And you, Bertie, an ex-nurse who has seen the bloody consequences of violence in the real world."

Perhaps wanting to steer Marion away from her preoccupation with the violence of online games, Bertie told her of Lisa's little episode the other day when, much to her concern, she had smuggled into the apartment some kind of headset that had certainly not yet seen the market.

"But what really got to me," she confided, remembering how Lisa had giggled and told her not to tell her dad, "was her assumption of my complicity. Of course, I would never tell Alex, but do you think she's pushing the envelope a bit too far? I mean, she could land herself in trouble, and her father's company too."

Lisa knew full well how secretive they were about their new products at Sarssein, and fearful of spies stealing their research data. Alex had once told Bertie that everyone on their team had been required to sign nondisclosure agreements attesting to their commitment to silence. Lisa had signed one too, a bat mitzvah present for her non–bat mitzvah, that confirmed her coming-of-age. Now, she had conveniently disregarded her promise of secrecy under the guise of Bertie being family.

An image of the scene she had witnessed yesterday remained lodged in her head. Lisa had looked like a mime performing in the space before her. For all intents and purposes, she had disappeared, like she existed on another plane, cut off from her grandmother, from the telephone, from the TV, from the doorbell. Standing on an island big enough for only one, she'd seemed to hear nothing other than what came through the headset. Bertie had walked around her where she stood in the middle of the living room and searched her face for some sign of what she experienced. Was that excitement or fear when the tips of her ears turned red? She had yanked her T-shirt.

"That's when she noticed me," she told Marion.

"I bet she was watching porn."

"No, just a Mardi Gras parade. She said it was lit and felt like she was right there in the middle of the throng with performers in front of her and others behind, and how they moved her along with them, dancing to this incredible salsa beat. She could feel their breath on her, the 3D was so real."

She remembered how flushed Lisa's face had looked, as if she had indeed participated in a boisterous parade.

"Of course, then I wanted to try it myself," she told Marion, oblivious of her own betrayal of secrecy, as she relayed what happened next. "But when I donned the thing over my head and the activities on the screen bombarded my senses, I felt totally dis...dis. What's that word again? You know...when you feel confused and don't know where you are."

Marion looked at her blankly, then suggested, "Dizzy?"

"No, no! Much more than dizzy. More like lost, bewildered."

Marion shrugged her shoulders. "Where is Lennie when we need him? He would know. He was such a wonk for words, that guy of yours."

He was that guy of hers. Momentarily, forgetting about the strangeness of what she'd experienced under the headset, she fell into the simplicity of the past. How much easier it was to recycle memories than negotiate new ideas. She used to call Lennie her word whisperer, because he could perform magic on her with words, and not only in bed. He chose his words like music, assessing them for their weight, their timbre, their nuance, and their rhythm. Did they balance smoothly? Did they make their point? It took her years to learn how to resist his magic.

For the latter part of his working life, Lennie had held the position of speech writer for the governor of British Columbia, where he practiced a different wizardry. He, of course, would have understood the appeal of online games. Lisa was still too young to play before he died, so Lennie never had the chance to explore them with her. But as a reader, he would have recognized the point of most games, given their basis in that oldest of literary tropes, the quest. A hero sets out to achieve or find something, and along the way defeats whatever stands between him and his goal. Who doesn't dream of being such a hero? Especially now with brave men as scarce as honest politicians and half the population believing the grail is not worth the effort to find.

"Discombobulated!" It suddenly came to Bertie. "That's what I was trying to say."

Between her and Marion, they often forgot words. They usually recalled them later, gratefully reassuring themselves they hadn't yet entered the steep chute to Alzheimer hell.

"Well, I am seventy-five," she reminded her friend, only to have Marion shake her head.

"Not until April, kiddo."

Being pedantic about numbers, Marion saw no need to age oneself. To her, numbers fixed the world and everything around it in its place. Otherwise, she said, we would all be free-floating and have no idea what was what.

"Anyway, this three-dimensional thing I was telling you about trying with Lisa," she continued, ignoring Marion's hairsplitting, "it is not the end."

"Uh-uh, you're getting that funny, twitchy smile on your face, Bertie, like you're about to explode. OK. What is it this time? What plan are you hatching?"

She uncrossed her legs, clad in black riding boots, and sat forward to listen. As far as Bertie knew, a draft horse pulling a Christmas carriage in the streets of Manhattan was the closest Marion had ever been to riding a horse.

"Well, this thing you put on your head gives you entrance to something called the metaverse that is supposed to be really complex."

"Meta-verse? You mean like Facebook's new name, Meta?"

"Facebook is only one of the companies developing metaverses. Lisa says Microsoft, Google, and other gaming concerns—Roblox, Epic, Doggle, whatever—are all in on it."

"And now Sarssein?"

"Shhh! Keep that to yourself!"

She looked around nervously, though there were few other customers in TechTown. The ones who were hunched up in their hoodies writing the Great American Novel on their laptops appeared oblivious of their surroundings.

"Nobody knows yet that Sarssein's involved," she whispered. "It's all very secretive, and you cannot breathe a word of it to anyone." She gripped Marion's wrists and made her swear. "Now that I know he's up to something new, I am not that surprised, as on a couple of occasions at our Friday-night dinners, I've heard him on the phone talking about something called the metaverse which meant nothing to me then."

"But now?"

"OK, it still means nothing," she admitted, feeling herself semantically handicapped despite Alex's explanations. "I'm clueless about the details, but Lisa says Sarssein is developing products for what her dad calls the third internet."

Marion had a way of turning her face sideways, digging her chin in, and then looking up with a frown. It was her skeptical look.

"What the hell is the third internet? And whatever happened to the second? I barely have a grip on the first." This, despite her love of numbers.

"None of us ever got interested in the second since TikTok and Instagram appeal mainly to kids, right?"

In fact, Facebook had hooked Bertie for a while until she realized its users' upbeat portrayals of their exciting lives could depress her as much as it did 14-year-olds. It was dispiriting enough seeing Martha Stewart at eighty-one posing in a bathing suit in *Sports Illustrated*; she didn't need to have her at the touch of a finger on her Facebook account.

"The point is," she continued, "we must get with it, Marion. We don't want to be left behind when the next Big Thing hits. Already kids younger than Lisa wait impatiently for the latest technological development while we elders remain totally unaware anything is even happening."

"So"—Marion tipped her cup to drain the last drop of her latte—"to use your Zoomer granddaughter's lingo, you are FOMO?"

"Yes, I fear missing out. Don't you? Remember how our age group always caught the wave before anyone else? Now we sip lattes while the revolution passes us by."

"I don't know. I was young then. Besides, there's a whole new lexicon out there and I don't understand a word of it."

"If we managed the language of the first internet, we'll ace the third. How hard can it be?"

"Would anyone even notice if we, say, failed to catch the wave, seeing we septuagenarians are invisible already?"

"But you remember how quickly our world became complex? Within a few years, you couldn't get on a bus, check out a library book, or pay for parking without interacting with a screen. The third internet may roll out at the same warp speed."

"And I may be pushing up daisies before then."

"We may well." Bertie joined her in that false laugh they always used when speaking of morbid things and which erupted from some border area in the brain where fear, sorrow, and laughter collided beyond their ability to keep them separate.

"I will find out more about it this Friday when I have dinner with the family, but from what Lisa told me—she says her dad talks to her about it because he likes to bounce ideas off her— the third internet will be some kind of virtual three-dimensional world, but unlike with the games I play with Lisa, you can build and control it yourself."

"So, you can make it whatever you want, then?"

"Yes. And act out your wildest fantasies in it."

"Whoa! I might like that."

"I thought you might."

"Oh, wait!" Suspicion stayed her smile. "This isn't going to be one of your sudden passions, is it? When you cajole me and Daru into some new project that interests you and then you dump it?"

"What do you mean?"

Bertie licked a few grains of hardened brown sugar from her coffee spoon, then wiped her mouth, as if she had no idea what Marion talked about. Behind the counter, Tom's fancy Gaggia machine with its triple spouts hissed and gurgled. The oven where he warmed croissants and bagels pinged, all of it together providing tonal accompaniment to their voices.

"Buying us librettos so we could sing arias from your favorite operas?"

"That was fun, though, wasn't it?"

"And what about the line dancing? And bird watching in the city? Remember too when you persuaded us that we needed to take this UW course about Romeo and Juliet in different cultures? And the one at the community college about postmodernism? And the Saturday morning class at the Asian Art Museum?"

"I'm curious about a lot of things," she fought back, miffed. "What's so terrible about having a variety of interests, even if they don't always turn out like I expect? Doesn't mean they aren't still enriching."

Sometimes, Marion could be so irritating, especially when she saw through Bertie's obfuscations and called her on them. Why couldn't she just go along with her ideas, give her some leeway, even if doing so were just an extension of their friendship? Did she have to be so honest? In Bertie's own periods of doubt that seemed to happen more frequently as the years passed, she sometimes wondered whether her myriad activities weren't willful insurance against mental loss, a way of staving off the inevitable. By constantly filling up with new knowledge, perhaps at some level, she hoped to compensate for the insidious leak that dripped out words, names, and dates, emptying her rusting tank of knowledge, and sending the data into the airstream like flotsam and jetsam, to be lost forever. In the years before Covid, when she had tried to study Spanish, it often felt that for every new Spanish word she gained, she lost an English one.

"I doubt Daru would be open to yet another one of your enthusiasms." Marion interrupted her unnerving thoughts. "Have you told her about the metaverse yet? I bet not. I suppose you thought you'd try it out on me first, so you didn't make a fool of yourself in front of her."

"So, look," she admitted to Marion, "maybe the metaverse is not the next Big Thing Lisa made it out to be. Maybe, it's all just hot air and the fuss will die down, and something even more exciting will displace it. Nevertheless, I am curious, aren't you?"

"I guess."

"Well, don't bowl me over with your enthusiasm!"

"It's just that...Aren't you even a little bit scared of getting involved with this stuff, Bertie? Maybe I'm being overly skeptic, but I don't trust these tech companies to look after my best interests. What if you really like acting out your...what was it?...your 'wildest fantasies?' What if you like it so much you don't want to leave, huh?" She elbowed Bertie until she smiled. "Just because it's the new thing, Old Bean, doesn't mean it is good for you."

"Says she, who always wants to try new things...new restaurants, new plays. Not that I'm complaining, Marion. I love that about you, how you are always the first to know about debut performances."

"Yeah, but debut technology? I'm out of my depth, Bertie."

"Me, too, but I'm not saying I'm going to *do* anything with the metaverse. I merely want to *ask* about it. Is the metaverse a game? Is it a movie? A hologram? What is it?" The café door opened and a group of four Chinese men dressed in suits ushered one another through, each more polite than the next, before descending on Tom with their coffee orders. The hoodies looked up for a minute, checked the men out, then returned to their laptops.

"I bet it's just another commercial product to fill a need we don't even know we have."

"Perhaps." Bertie hesitated, reluctant to reduce the whole exciting idea down to dollars and cents.

Around them on the walls of TechTown Café hung the art of their times: technology aestheticized. Framed abstractions of what might be circuit boards, numbers, and code, all of it colorful and beautiful, gave the nod to the café's techie neighborhood. Below the picture opposite her, the words "Created from Algorithm" differentiated it from the others, indicating, she guessed, that it was the outcome of complex directions sent to a computer, though she could be wrong. Neither she nor Marion had ever learned to code, so they were at a distinct disadvantage. She wished Daru had joined them for coffee, but she was still home, tending to her sick husband, Aditya, whose needs seemed to increase by the day. Being ten years younger than them, Daru claimed ease with the basic instructions of writing code and could have enlightened them. Even she, however, might have been at a loss to explain the Rumpelstiltskin-like conversion of straw into gold. How does a string of numbers produce beauty and whatever it is that transforms those numbers into art?

"I don't know, Marion," Bertie finally admitted. "I'm confused too. Perhaps the metaverse is just a whole other world, something so different, there aren't ordinary words to explain it."

They sat for a moment in silence, aware of their ignorance. That's the thing about getting old. You become more cognizant of what you don't know, which she supposed you could say is wisdom. Anyway, there was nothing left to tell. She didn't know anything more about the metaverse, and even if she could remember everything Lisa had told her, she couldn't explain it. So, the two of them returned their cups to the bussing station. Then, stepping out from the intoxicating aromas of Ethiopian, Columbian, Costa Rican, and Hawaiian roasts, they made their way back through the mist to their apartment building, Bertie imagining what this new hyped-up world could be, and Marion wondering how she could rein in her inquisitive pal before she went off on another one of her unexpected tangents, and dragged her best friends kicking and screaming behind.

# CHAPTER 3

—

ARIELLE AND ALEX LIVED IN A QUIET NEIGHBORHOOD near Lake Washington, far from Sarssein and a good distance from Arielle's practice on Sandpoint near Seattle Children's Hospital. Both hungered for quiet at the end of their busy days, so they maintained a serene home, allowing only Chopin and Schubert—turned to low volume—ever to disturb their calm. In their house, CCR didn't stand a chance, at least not at night, although Bertie sometimes heard rap in her daughter's car before she quickly turned down the sound. Arielle's affinity for hip-hop struck an incongruous note in her otherwise predictable tastes, a rhythmic ripple in the well-ordered life she lived with Alex in their remodeled craftsman house.

Despite it still being November, many larger homes in their neighborhood already showcased their Christmas lights. During Covid, a thriving industry stringing holiday lights had arisen among the recently unemployed, who together with other gig workers (dog walkers, house-number painters, mobile car cleaners, and food deliverers) courted busy people in the area with their offers of hassle-free services. Those other unemployed men and women who hadn't yet found workable ideas for earning money and were often homeless rarely graced the Madrona streets. Instead, they congregated downtown, where they could find shelters, food banks, and unemployment offices. The problem of homelessness perplexed everyone in Seattle. None of the answers seemed to work.

Being aware of how easily middle-class women, especially the divorced, single, and widowed, could slip between the cracks, she and Marion empathized with the vulnerable. One day you could be shopping at Lindstrom, the next discovering that your deceased husband, the bastard, had left you with nothing but bills. Marion's immigrant parents struggling to make it in the new country had protected her from the New York streets by constantly reminding her that if she didn't study and do her homework, she would end up on those very streets. Though even as a child she understood their fearmongering as derived from their own insecurity, it left her with the constant need to check her financial well-being.

"What if I lose my job? What if I catch a debilitating disease? What if the banks fail?"

She would go on and on, each possibility feeding her anxiety until Bertie reassured her she would take her in and see that she didn't land on the streets, though of course her own situation could be equally vulnerable. Insecurity was the name of the game; the nature of capitalism that kept you on your toes.

But what to do about those bereft of house and home? How was one to deal with the numbers of people holing up in doorways and alcoves or under the freeways? To assuage their guilt at being relatively privileged, she and Marion donated food to the local food banks and, when they came across indigent women, even those who wore their attitudes on their skins with tattoos that told onlookers to eff themselves, often stopped to hear their life stories. What did they need that she and Marion could provide?

Sometimes, however, being old and carrying a purse made the two of them seem like easy prey. Once, a young man named Phil, battling the dragons in his mind, attacked Marion and she ended up in the ER with multiple contusions. But Marion had long been a tough broad. A few bumps would not deter her from doing what was needed, and within a week of leaving the hospital, she and Bertie were back on the streets dribbling their ameliorative drops into this immense sea of woe.

When Bertie arrived at the family's home for their regular Friday-night dinner, Lisa at first hid her own bumpy contusion.

"What happened, sweetheart?"

Bertie pulled her hair back behind her ears, revealing a big bump on her forehead that measured at least two inches across.

"Nothing," she said, avoiding her gran's eyes.

"Nobody tells me anything." Alex in his black turtleneck lifted his shoulders and deferred to his wife. Though he was the co-founder of Sarssein, he dressed like Steve Jobs.

"Mom, can you help me dish out?"

Arielle took the apple and walnut cake Bertie had brought for dessert and beckoned her to follow her to the kitchen, from where enticing smells wafted and a litany of beeps signaled the oven had switched off. Wearing silicone gloves, her daughter slid a laden tray from the oven. She was into sheet-pan cooking, and this one contained salmon, asparagus, and mushrooms spread out on foil that you could dispose of afterward. Arielle had always been Miss Organized. She needed to be, what with her responsibilities as doctor, wife, and mother. Now, she stood leaning against a kitchen cabinet looking weighed down by what she bore on her shoulders. Below her daughter's lovely teal eyes, grayish crescents hung like sagging flags.

"Lisa punched some boy at school."

Bertie knew immediately who the boy was.

Arielle crossed her arms tightly around herself as if she feared expanding beyond the dotted lines. Lisa, she informed her, had smacked her schoolmate on the nose hard enough to make it bleed. The kids had been in a tussle over Lisa's binder, the one in which she worked out her math problems before transferring the answers online. When he tried to seize it, she socked him, and he responded by grabbing the heavy binder from her and whacking her across the head with it. Who would have thought pugilistic parity between the sexes would start so young? Whatever happened to gentlemanly behavior toward females, at least in public?

"That's the downside of gender equality," Bertie said, making light of the incident to avoid adding to Arielle's woes. Her daughter's knitted eyebrows thrust up anxiety lines that even Botox could not have relaxed.

"Do you think these violent online games are making Lisa more aggressive?"

Bertie hugged her daughter, telling her to stop worrying, and reassured her Lisa would be fine. She had learned long ago not to offer her opinion on anything that might reflect on Arielle's or Alex's handling of their daughter. She was sensitive that way, Arielle, despite her confidence. Once, when during Lisa's infancy Bertie had made what she thought an innocent remark about projectile vomiting, she had turned on her, demanding that she not tell her what to do with her own child when pediatrics was her job. Surely, she knew what was best for children.

Ever since that conversation, Bertie had kept her mouth shut, becoming "granny zipped lips" all the way.

Remembering Lisa's earlier computer outburst about Jared, she wondered about Arielle's question. Did the games she played affect Lisa negatively? Did they affect her? Was she becoming more aggressive? It seemed the more she played, the easier it became to cauterize her enemy with a ray gun and incise a simpering druid with her saber. An explosion that sent limbs flying like scattered feathers into outer space sped up her pulse not at all.

Back at the table, over the flickering Shabbat candles—the one ritual their secular family still observed—Alex reassured them that games did not make players aggressive. They served as safety valves, he said, as he picked up a spear of asparagus with his fingers and chomped off the end.

"Like those explicit manga in Japan, they ventilate frustration, reducing real violence."

She hoped he was right. Did the Japanese have statistics to prove it?

She listened to the technical banter between Lisa and her dad, noting how it connected them and brought them close. It was their way of communicating, she realized. Of checking in with each other. Most of their conversation flew by her, making no sense at all, and when they started using acronyms—MMORPG, NPC, PvP, MEMS, or some such—they could have been speaking a foreign language. She looked at Arielle. Did her daughter understand this three-dimensional stuff? She had described to her earlier how surgeons at Children's Hospital sometimes used 3D when performing certain operations.

To Bertie's relief, Lisa eventually found talking in acronyms exhausting. She started percussing the table edge with her fingers, like she'd seen her mother do on patients. In desperation, she pulled her phone from her jean pocket.

"No texting at the table." Arielle pounced on the phone and placed it with the other three Apples in the wooden fruit bowl on the sideboard. Except for the occasional "new text" clicks, they lay there silenced, metal rectangles of information that were finger-smudged, dented, and nicked. From across the room, amid an array of family photos, Lennie smiled on the four of them separated from their control centers.

"But I don't want to listen anymore to Dad going on about immersive 3D. Sorry, Dad," she said, offering him an apologetic smile. "As fascinated as I am by all this stuff, you can become quite boring when you get on your hobbyhorse."

Humor eluded Alex, nuance too. When he regaled them with a joke as he often tried to do, Lisa would shout, "Lame!" but Arielle would laugh anyway out of wifely loyalty and touch his arm. Whatever held those two together, it worked; they had been married for fourteen years. At first, Bertie had been surprised at Arielle's choice of husband, given the many handsome, talented doctors she worked with. Not that Alex wasn't pleasant looking and intelligent himself, but a Casanova he was not. Turned out his very lack of romantic experience had attracted her daughter. She appreciated he made no moves on her.

"There was something so innocent about him, so straightforward," she once told her mother. He just came out with it one day and said to her, "I love you and want to marry you and have children with you." And that was that!

"Well," Bertie said to Lisa, "I *would* like to know more about immersive 3D and also"—she turned to Alex—"about that thing called the metaverse. In South Lake Union, around our apartment block, I often hear the word bandied about. What does it all mean, Alex?"

Lisa groaned. "OK, OK, you guys talk and I'll just…"

To her mother's amazement, she offered to do the dishes, even though it was not her turn until Sunday.

With her departure and enthused by Bertie's interest, Alex dropped the acronyms. From his Pandora's box mind in which the weird and wonderful swarmed continuously, and strings of numbers and words lay entwined in strange, complicated formations, he pulled one string at a time to show her what, to his mind, couldn't be clearer: The metaverse developed by Microsoft and Meta resembled the online worlds she saw in the games she and Lisa played. Only, the metaverse wasn't just a game. There were no ferocious demons and dragons pursuing you, unless that was what you wanted. It was another meta-world, a parallel one made up of numerous worlds you could enter and leave at will.

"But what do Microsoft and Meta mean by that?" she asked, carefully guarding her words so she didn't let slip she knew about Sarssein's secret project. "How many worlds are there?"

"As many as you want. Hundreds, and still more created every day. Also"—he carefully pulled out another singular string—"instead of joining someone else's metaverse, you can create your own personal one."

When she asked what people did in their parallel worlds, he explained it in straightforward language that through their avatars, they could do whatever they felt like—dance, fight, argue, pray, shop, share dirty jokes. And they could do it with any avatar they wanted, provided it was live and willing to interact.

"So, there are unlive characters too?"

"Sure. Being unconnected, the unlive characters waited to be claimed by players and brought to life."

When she asked how a player recognized the live from the unlive sitting in the waiting room, as it were, Alex took her literally, explaining that the unlive were not sitting but wandering the metaverse like dead souls in Bardo. Wow! That was a hot simile for Alex, who normally stuck to concrete facts. Yet Arielle had once confided to her he secretly wrote poetry. Not free verse, of course, because that would have been pushing it for a techie who worked in structured code.

"Wearing the VR headset," he explained further, "you see through the avatar's eyes as if you were him or her in a three-dimensional world, able to look all around you, including behind. You become part of whatever's going on. You become immersed in it."

So that was what Lisa had meant by "immersive 3D." She made the connections, wondering at the same time if there didn't exist an ethics of looking. After all, it didn't sound kosher to look through somebody else's eyes as if they were your own, even if that person wasn't live. Yet, walking in someone else's shoes, people said, encouraged empathy, just as reading novels did. But literally seeing through someone's eyes?

Remembering her single moment wearing the headset Lisa had brought to the apartment—and which her granddaughter had assured her she had returned to her father's office—she had felt no empathy for the Mardi Gras marchers and could only recall the dizziness she experienced. If she had stayed marching in the same parade, she would certainly have toppled over her avatar. Was that even possible, falling over your avatar? Or would you separate, your avatar staying in the virtual world, you in the real? Could you have one foot in each? She imagined herself sending her avatar sprawling, apologizing profusely, then realizing she talked only to herself. This network of 3D virtual worlds certainly sounded more sophisticated than the games they played, and she struggled to visualize it.

To impress her son-in-law and show him she wasn't completely out of it—Bertie sometimes wondered if he thought she was losing it when she couldn't remember a word—she asked how real the parallel worlds looked. Would it be like watching a documentary at the Science Center's IMAX theater, with its surround sound and screens?

"As real as the real thing," Alex effused. "A metaverse can reproduce the real world exactly, and at an exact time, down to the tiniest detail. I tell you, Bertie, being in this parallel world will be revolutionary. It could change your life forever!"

Whether she wanted her life to change forever begged the question, and what did forever mean to her, anyway? How many years? But curiosity had always got the better of her, so she continued to listen as, sliding out yet another new string, Alex explained how you could choose the realm where you wanted to interact and, depending on "the platform" used, even build it yourself, buying the virtual bricks and virtual infrastructure with virtual money.

"Why would I want to buy things that weren't real?"

"Think of the books you have on your iPad. You pay for them, and you can read them any time, but you can't physically touch them. In the metaverse, it will be the same. Your avatar can buy digital clothes and digital bicycles, or whatever you choose, but unlike the books on your iPad, you can sell them in the metaverse using cryptocurrency."

"So, then, it is all about commerce and the sale of virtual products?"

Like the lovable, eccentric guy he was, Alex didn't read the skepticism on her face and continued. "That, plus advertising and data collection. It will be a parallel plane of existence on top of our digital and physical economies."

Arielle, however, recognized her mother's look and immediately told her how just a couple of years ago Reporters Without Borders had constructed brick-by-brick an Uncensored Library in 3D that allowed users in countries like Russia, Saudi Arabia, and Egypt to read banned literature. Her daughter knew where Bertie's sympathies lay.

Not to be outdone, Alex then got his spin on about what this new technology could do in education, engineering, and health. Bertie still had lots of questions, but when he explained that the metaverse was just one stop on a mixed-reality spectrum and even more exciting states of virtuality lay ahead of them, she held up her hands.

"Enough!" She had hit overload mode.

Luckily, Lisa returned just then.

"Done!"

The conversation switched to the midterm elections and whether they would be washed away by the Red Wave of conspiracy theorists and election deniers.

By the time she got home to Mariela Plaza, it was already 10:30, but Michael still stood at his post, his head stuck in *Science*, an open Diet Coke alongside him. She would probably not have interrupted his concentration, but just then that sweet young couple, Phillip and David from apartment 2820, exited the elevator and called out "Goodnight, Michael," blowing him a kiss which he theatrically blew back to them. When they disappeared through the doors, she asked him whether he thought the metaverse would be the next Big Thing.

"The metaverse is just hype," he said, closing the journal but keeping a finger in it to mark his place.

"But my son-in-law says it is so exciting!"

"Maybe." He rubbed his thumb and forefinger along the line of small gold rings affixed to the edge of his right ear. "But all I hear is a lot of promises. These big companies, Mrs. Glazer, they keep telling us this virtual fantasyland will be here any day now, only to postpone the announcement because of glitches. Three-dimensionality, immersive experience, interoperability, synchronicity, they can't get any of it right."

While she now knew what some of Michael's words meant, she had a long way to go.

"'Not enough bandwidth and too much latency,' they say; "not enough computing power." And then there's the problem of enough servers. It's an enormously complex project that needs so many components, and each built by a competing company."

Then he smiled at her, as if sharing inside info on the stock market, and told her not to hold her breath. It was anyone's guess, he said, if the metaverse would ever get off the ground.

Back in the apartment, she sat for a moment staring at her computer, this simple-looking machine that had already changed so many lives and which stood poised one day to produce ever more mysterious technological tools that they would learn to use without ever truly understanding their workings but trusting their creators to protect them. The problem was she might need that protection sooner rather than later, in fact, in six months if her son-in-law came through with his guarded promise.

At the end of dinner, Alex and Lisa had decided that, given Bertie's curiosity and enthusiasm, a metaverse specially designed for her would be a wonderful seventy-fifth birthday present. If Alex could convince his colleagues it would be worth their while to approve the idea—and it was a big "if"—he and the Sarssein team would create a special three-dimensional realm in which she would have a virtual play space to act out anything that tickled her fancy. The choice of place, music, people, and most importantly her avatar, would be up to her. By April, he promised, she would have her magical realm. Maybe not in a box tied with a red ribbon, but custom made and ready for her to enter.

That night, a music worm looping around her head kept her awake, tossing and turning, suspicious of the emperor's new clothes:

*The King is in the altogether...*

# CHAPTER 4

———

"CHOOSE A PLACE, GRAN," AS THOUGH IT WERE A DONE deal that Bertie would be on the receiving end of her own bespoke metaverse. In fact, the chances of Alex persuading his secretive partner and colleagues to his idea still lay in the realm of a miracle. All Alex had offered her was a tentative agreement, so she could think about what she might like to do if given the opportunity.

It had been Lisa who had first brought up the idea, two weeks ago at dinner, only to have it smashed down by her father. He reminded her of Sarssein's need for secrecy. No way would he allow their products out of the house, what with all the spies lurking around, ready to steal technical information wherever they could gain access. From Lisa and Alex's conversation, Bertie realized although her son-in-law had not admitted it in so many words, Sarssein was as deeply involved in the metaverse competition as Microsoft and Meta. The only difference was nobody outside of Sarssein knew it, except Lisa. And what she knew, or rather suspected, was that her dad's top-secret company possessed incredible technological advancements related to mixed reality that they were hiding from prying eyes in the bowels of their South Lake Union building.

So, with the negotiating skills she had absorbed from her grandfather, along with the blunt edge of reason, her father's favored method of dispute, Lisa pulled apart Alex's argument about secrecy. How could Sarssein have hoped to get any products right when nobody but nerdy techies in the company had access to them? Wasn't that why so many companies had to recall products or add fixes when stuff turned out wrong? And, why were tech instructions for the public so badly written and simply unreadable?

Alex remained unmoved. "I said no."

"But Dad…"

"No, Lisa."

"But techies do not know what ordinary people need, or what they understand. They see everything through their own skill sets."

Alex hesitated, then conceded just a little. "It is certainly true a need exists for all demographics to try Sarssein products, but…"

That admission was all Lisa needed. Seeing her opening, she jumped in with, "What if the situation could be quid pro quo between Sarssein and Gran? Gran could try out the new product, satisfy her curiosity, and give feedback to Sarssein on what worked for her and what didn't. That way, both sides would benefit, wouldn't they?" She looked at her father, like the 13-cum-23-year-old she alternated between.

Alex rose from his chair and walked in circles around the dinner table, his hands clasped in front of him, his thumbs knocking rhythmically against each other as his mind navigated its way through the obstacles he would confront at Sarssein. Foremost among them were his co-director and colleagues, who considered contact with any outsider risky business. He did too, usually, but Bertie was an old woman, as Lisa had reminded him. What harm could she do in her virtual world?

"Well," he began, "maybe if I could get Bertie into a user-research study..."

And that was how they had left it that night, a maybe. Today, however, Lisa acted as if it were a done deal that everything would fall into place and that her gran would get her magical realm, though Bertie had heard nothing from Alex since then.

"Well, what would *you* choose if your dad gave you your own realm?" she asked now, not wanting to get her hopes up, but willing to play along with her granddaughter. Lisa had been sulking recently because Alex refused to let her loose in the metaverse with her own realm. Neither of them had mentioned the actual headset, so Bertie assumed Lisa had returned it without Alex knowing it had left the house. It's not that he didn't trust her alone in the metaverse; he had explained it was the other people out there, the ones who took advantage of children who made him fear for her.

"But I'm thirteen, Dad. I know how to look after myself."

"You know how to punch," Bertie corrected her.

She giggled. "You should have seen Jared's face."

"I can imagine, but that explosion of yours...and I realize how satisfying it must have been...earned you a bump on the head and an afternoon in detention."

"It was worth it. When Dad eventually offers me a realm, I can take boxing lessons to perfect my punch." A mischievous grin flittered across her face. "No harm being prepared."

She sprawled across the brown sofa, one socked leg dangling over the edge. When she wasn't at the computer, she hung out on the stained old sofa, her favorite place. Bertie had tried to get rid of it numerous times, but her granddaughter insisted that nothing new could be quite as comfortable.

"Actually," she said, twirling a loose thread from the cushion beneath her, "the realm I would really like, if I could choose, is Dazzleland. Remember when you and Gramps took me there for my birthday? We had so much fun together on the rides. It was awesome."

"How your grandfather kept up with you...racing from one attraction to the next...like some windup toy."

"To be honest, he was cheugy. He pretended to be cool when anyone could see the sudden dives and swoops made him want to vomit."

She laughed fondly, remembering how Lennie had braved his own fear. Then, with a sage nodding of her head, she concluded that in the end he'd done pretty well.

"I mean, after all, he was an old man!"

Bertie assured her she knew that.

The childlike delight in her memories of that day eventually faded and as she reluctantly returned to reality, her face grew still.

"I know it wouldn't be the same now, of course. I'm much too old for that kind of thing."

Bertie nodded. Didn't she know full well that you could never go back home, never relive an experience in the same way. Now that lesson had forced itself on Lisa and it proved sobering. Yes, we were all too old for silly rides, she thought.

Sometimes, Lisa confounded her when she jumped so quickly between child and adult musings. One moment Bertie would be chattering away to a sweet sentimental girl, the next conversing with a wise young woman coming to terms with her own insights. Lisa half lay on the sofa now, swinging one leg back and forth, a metronome beating the rhythm of her thoughts. She said nothing and Bertie wondered where her mind took her.

Then, with a sad smile, her granddaughter added, "It wouldn't be the same without him there, would it?"

Bertie sat down on the sofa next to her and kissed her on the head where the bump had receded and left a blue bruise the size of a small Post-it note.

"You really loved him, didn't you?"

Lisa caught her top lip between her teeth, then jumped up, changing the subject.

"Time to play *King of Avalon*!" She plonked herself in front of the computer and pulled up the screen. "I bet I'll be King Arthur's replacement this time. No way will you build a bigger power base," she challenged Bertie.

"Perhaps. But wait till you see my dragon. It will do anything I say."

And they were off, building, protecting, threatening, and asserting. In between, they stabbed, shot, and splattered with blood. Bertie wondered if her behavior transitions confused Lisa too.

She knew Avalon was not where her granddaughter wanted to be, nor Dazzleland, for that matter. If Alex had given Lisa her choice of realms, she would have requested a nightclub. For the last two years, she had played clarinet in her school's jazz band and had surprised them all with her dedication. Every afternoon at the apartment, she would dutifully practice, in the process becoming good enough to join the older students in the school's band.

In a nightclub where nobody knew her, she had once told Bertie, she could play the music as her gut felt it, not as the band director instructed her. Lennie had loved jazz too, and sometimes when Lisa spent the afternoon at the apartment, she would take out his old CDs and they would sit together on the couch and listen to Count Basie or Duke Ellington.

To get back to *her* realm, the one Lisa wanted her to decide on, Bertie had a bucket list of places she hoped to visit before she croaked: India, Egypt, Sardinia, Scotland, Senegal…Somehow, they felt safer to her, more familiar perhaps, than this unknown online place that didn't exist in real time. Well, it did exist, but it wasn't the real one she would enter, just its twin she could alter, destroy, or populate with mythical gods who would feed her blueberries and lull her to sleep with ostrich feathers.

By now, she had become familiar with the gaming world's possibilities and could maneuver herself all over the screen in a game created by somebody else, but at the game's conclusion, someone, something, AI perhaps, switched her off and shut her out. At the back of her mind, she always felt reassured a puppet master ultimately controlled the game even when she thought herself most in control. So, the idea of being fully in charge of a world that wasn't even really there filled her with trepidation. When she confessed her fear to Alex, however, he dismissed it, explaining that if the project materialized, his team would keep tabs on her. They would report back to him, though he personally would not track her movements or watch her avatar. The only other people who would see what she got up to in her secret place were the avatar controllers who entered her realm.

"So," he added, "feel free to kick up a storm or whatever it is you want to do in your 3D world."

Bertie laughed, half apologetic for being such a wuss. "So, I am responsible for everything that happens in my online world?"

"Sure. Enjoy your power."

"Go for it, Gran. Take the Red Pill."

To Lisa, Bertie's life must have looked so boring. Same old, same old. Her friends were Marion and a slighter younger woman, Daru Chowdhury, the two she called "the aunties." As in Indian culture, the aunties watched over Lisa and had no compunction about scolding her in Bertie's absence if they saw her do anything inappropriate or unsafe. They looked out for her interests, and she could turn to any of them for help. They were her village, she, a beloved child. But that was what made them boring, Bertie supposed. It was a different boring from Lisa's parents perhaps, who spent their lives at work, but humdrum, nevertheless. Personally, they thought of themselves as *The Golden Girls*, women of a certain age who were perhaps not funny like the originals. How did Blanche, Rose, and Dorothy come up smiling every day? It made Bertie wonder if old people had to be amusing to attract interest. No doubt Marion would have answered that last question with, "Of course! That's how we protect the young from the reality of it all." Hmmm, she didn't know. Old age certainly wasn't a laugh a minute, but the girls often had a ball together.

Even so, what did the three of them do whenever they got together and had the freedom to launch themselves into any wonderous activity of their choice? They talked, talked, talked! About the fighting in Ukraine; about the race for the 2024 presidency; about Nancy Pelosi stepping down from her House leader seat. Sometimes they drank coffee with the talk, other times wine, but whatever the beverage, the conversation circled around politics and the Orange Man threatening all things they believed precious. Politics reminded them their passion lay alive and well just below their wrinkled surfaces. Sometimes they attended the theater or the symphony or the opera, but at this point in Lisa's life, those places represented more ho-hum boredom. *What do you do for excitement?*

So, here lay Bertie's opportunity to step out of her comfort zone. She wanted to say yes to life. "OK," she said to Lisa, trying to come up with a place that might sound exciting, but was not so far out of her realm of experience that she would feel lost.

She had no wish to explore outer space, for instance, nor did she desire to spelunk in airless caves, or search the seafloor to befriend an octopus. She knew she didn't want to climb a mountain in Kenya, go on a safari in South Africa, ski a steep slope in Switzerland, parachute over the Amazon jungle, parasail…

"But it won't be you," Lisa reminded her. "You won't be the one in danger. Only your avatar will be in danger."

"But I will kill her off on the first day if I do any of those things. Won't I be responsible for her decisions?"

"It's just make-believe, Gran," Lisa reassured her, as Bertie had so often reassured her granddaughter's younger self when fairy-tale witches made her clutch her grandmother's arm.

"OK," she said again, determined to make a decision. "But seeing this is my first time, what if I choose a place closer to home, like Venice Beach or Los Angeles," she said, forgetting her earlier words to Lisa about the impossibility of reliving the past.

Lisa looked at her as if she had relinquished all hope of extracting her gran from her boring life.

● ●

In 2022, Venice Beach was anything but boring. It barely differed from Seattle in its number of homeless people and its depressed state. Ramshackle tents constructed from plastic and metal sheeting now lined Ocean Front Walk, and empty alcohol bottles and garbage lay strewn around them on the warm white sand. Where previously free-spirited pot users had made love in the sun, now drug-addled violent men fought one another and broke into neighboring houses rooting for cash. Though people still used the beach as in the seventies for bicycling, skating, and people-watching, it was no longer safe.

In 1974, LA had been an exciting place to Bertie, a Pandora's box of unknown possibilities. She had just divorced her first husband, having married young on the assumption compatible pheromones made marriage inevitable. It hadn't taken her long to discover that he and she shared nothing more than sex and she had quickly disentangled herself, grateful that her little pill had protected her from bringing children into their unhappy world of two. Soon after, in the hope of recovering from her mistaken choice of partner and also from the real pressures of her nursing job, she spent a couple weeks in the Venice Beach sunshine with her friend and nursing colleague, Christine.

When Christine and Bertie graduated from Boston U, the Vietnam War had gripped their country in its increasingly tight and bloody maw. Demonstrations had started, and the two women were right there with the protesters, screaming their disgust for this capitalist war, as they saw it then.

The Kent State massacre still lay in the future, but even without that marker, they already feared the direction their government was taking them. No way would they work for the Man, they decided. Instead, they would serve their fellow Americans. They would care for the people who had been sent to fight in this impossible mess, nursing them back to health at one of the Veteran Administration hospitals. Would-be Florence Nightingales filled with noble intentions and armed with syringes and blood-pressure cuffs, they went to battle at the VA's West Roxhill campus.

After an intense five years of caring for the sick, and repairing the wounded physically but also mentally—the Left still gave them the finger for being a part of the imbroglio—Bertie needed to put down her lantern, if only for a fortnight, in LA.

So what if at seventy-five she couldn't go back? So what if she couldn't recapture that same sense of freedom and irresponsibility? If her metaverse materialized after running the gauntlet at Sarssein, a simulacrum with fun highlights, she thought, would be just fine.

●●

The promise of this new interaction and involvement in the metaverse thrilled Bertie. The Covid shutdown had been hard on them all and, after Lennie's death, she had spiraled into a depression. Stuck at home in her sweats and slippers, she saw no reason to get dressed. Marion and Daru slumped around in the same state of sartorial lethargy. She moved back and forth between the TV and her computer where she occasionally set up or received a Zoom call. The three of them comprised their own Circle of Trust, limiting their contact to their immediate families, but they yearned for interaction with the outside world, to be part again of that great throbbing crowd at the market shouting, "Throw the fish!" Covid had shrunk their lives that were already shrunk, husbands gone, careers over, looks faded, but they had one another and a sense of humor, at least enough to keep them afloat, to keep them laughing even if their laughs were tinged with sadness. Sometimes, perhaps only occasionally, they filled them with joy.

Though she was infinitely grateful for Daru and Marion, it was Lisa who ultimately saved her from the edge.

"Don't cry, Gran. You still have me."

She did indeed. Although Lisa's school hadn't reopened, she had a lesson plan to follow, and online discussions with her teachers and other students in her class. Every afternoon, Bertie had to be there for her, eyes dry, no whimpering, sucking it up so she could encourage her as she manipulated split screens, researched material, cut and pasted, oftentimes having to adjust her expectations as screens failed or students' computers crashed. Every resolved problem taught her something—patience, persistence, and technical know-how—and as she learned, so did Bertie.

At this point, she and Lisa started playing the online games that would become such an integral part of her life.

In the end, they mourned Lennie together. After her homework had been done, they allowed themselves to think about him, talk about him, and listen to his favorite jazz pieces. Drinking his favorite tea in the rose-covered teacups, they could almost see him there across the table, his cup cradled in his hand, his dimple winking at them, his favorite people in the world.

# CHAPTER 5

___

IT WAS TOO COLD TO GO OUTSIDE. MOUNT RAINIER shrouded in white clouds peered down in disappointment on the Seattleites who no longer revered and worshipped it. On the west side of their top-floor conservatory, however, the sun shone through the enclosed verandah's curved glass, warming Marion, Daru, and Bertie where they lay like TB patients in a Swiss sanatorium. Except for the occasional airplane leaving its contrail spoor across the arced heavens, nothing marred their view of the Olympic Mountains until the snow clouds drifted east and enveloped their building. They were thirty floors up and lay alongside one another in a row on those flat loungers you find on cruise ships or around swimming pools. Among the three of them, they possessed two rebuilt knees and a new hip, plus numerous dermatological scorch marks on necks and chests. You would think they had survived torture by cigarette burns.

At eleven in the morning, they were the only people in the place. On one side of Marion's lounger, she had dumped her enormous black purse. What she kept in it, she never revealed, but it bulged enough that Bertie wondered if it bore an emergency change of clothes. Since Bertie carried her own bulging bag stuffed with emergency pharmaceuticals, she could not comment. But then, there was also Marion's black cloak, which lay in a tangled pile at the foot of her lounger. In a play on the young Harry Potter's artifact, they called it Marion's magical cloak of visibility because, when they were out in public and she wanted to make her presence felt, she would sometimes swirl it like an eighteenth-century dandy, and they would half expect her to draw her sword from between its formidable folds.

"If you don't have talent, beauty, or youth," she'd say, "you must be flamboyant. It is the only way to catch attention."

"But what if you don't have enough spunk to be outrageous?" Daru once asked.

"At least wear outsize glasses like *Vogue* magazine's Anna Wintour."

Daru, when Bertie told her about the metaverse, understood her curiosity immediately.

"Of course, I feel the need to be at the center of the universe," she shared. "Why shouldn't I? For most of our lives, the world has revolved around *our* values, *our* music, *our* clothing, *our* drugs, and even *our* language. It's natural to miss it. Just because we are old, I mean old-ish, doesn't mean we don't yearn to be part of the 'it' thing again."

Bertie was so grateful to hear Daru empathize that point, she leaned over to give her a hug, only to hear her continue, "Even so, I am no fool, Bertie. I'm not ready to be the first to jump into the metaverse quicksand. *Where angels fear to tread,* and all that."

"So, what? You would rather watch me sink first?"

Still, now that her metaverse looked as if it would materialize, Bertie appreciated even that bit of understanding. Her intrepid son-in-law had finally convinced his Sarssein team to include her in one of their user-research studies, even though consumers in the sixty-five to eighty-five demographic hardly constituted a major market, but of course its share could grow with product familiarity, and wasn't that what Sarssein hoped, she'd asked him?

On the many pieces of paper that laid out the company's rules and protocols for participation, followed by bulleted lists of the penalties for transgressing them, she had signed her name, conscious of the enormity of doing so. The problem was that unbeknownst to Alex although not to Lisa, she had already shared her plans with Daru and Marion and couldn't renege or deny them. Her friends would recognize immediately that she lied. Besides, she needed them for support as she entered this new experience that lay so far outside of her everyday world. Knowing there could be no backing out, her best option, she thought, was to have them swear fidelity to her "no-talk" demand. In fact, she forced them to sign a contract, promising her they would never speak of it to anyone other than to Bertie. Despite neither woman being a loose cannon, there was still a chance that Alex's competitors might overhear something one of them said, potentially outsmarting her son-in-law and pushing him out of the company, resulting in the loss of his stock options. As for her, she would be toast and her relationship with her son-in-law kaput. For all she knew, should such a catastrophe happen, Alex might even turn Lisa against her. That was a possibility she could not bear to imagine.

Since she didn't dare tell Alex now, her only path lay forward. So, she sat up, pushed her fears to the back of her mind, and announced to Marion and Daru the venue she had chosen for her personal metaverse.

"Venice Beach in 1974!"

Marion looked shocked. "Isn't that a bit like using a tool for the future to return to the past? Sounds regressive to me."

"Also, you're unlikely to have a good Sartre or Heidegger discussion there," Daru added. She had been a literature major.

"I am not looking to discuss either! Don't rush to judgment. You never know what musclemen and sun worshippers read."

Bertie adjusted the back of the lounger. She could never get comfortable with these things. They were either too flat or too erect and she'd sometimes hurt her fingers when she tried to alter their angle.

"Besides, I wanted somewhere superficial. The whole idea of the metaverse seems to me a lot of hype and bling."

Even as she said the words, she realized she indirectly criticized her own son-in-law. Hadn't he explained how many component levels it took to create that outer skin, the one the public saw? Simplicity was complex, he had insisted.

"On the other hand," Daru remarked, scrolling through her iPhone, and showing her she'd finished the *NYT* Wordle quiz in three tries when she knew very well it had taken Bertie five.

"Venice Beach does have a slightly grunge/glamorous sound about it, which could be fun. After all, we are talking about a game, aren't we?"

"Yes, that's all it is, a silly game," Bertie said despite Alex telling her it wasn't a game but a world in which to live and act.

She sat up, rubbing her back which ached between the fourth and fifth vertebrae. Though she, Marion, and Daru exposed their aches and pains to one another, they tried unsuccessfully to keep them hidden from everybody else, especially young people, so they wouldn't be reminded of what lay ahead. Still, it was one thing to imitate Blanche, Rose, and Dorothy who represented old age on-screen as one ball of fun, but quite another to live it, especially given that Bertie was closer in age to Dorothy's mother, Sophia.

"All I'm asking of you," she said, turning to each of her friends, "is your input on my avatar. I want suggestions. How should she look? What kind of personality should she have?"

"Hang on a sec, I have to answer this."

Daru got up and moved to the end of the room to take a phone call. She held the phone away from her ear with a grimace and they heard a man's raised voice: "I thought we were having lunch together."

When she returned to them, she sighed. "Aditya."

She was the only one of them who still had a husband, a sick one whose mind pickled in pain-killing drugs could not keep the days straight, and in his confusion would make demands of her which she always tried to fulfill. She would join him later for lunch.

Meanwhile, Marion had been thinking about Bertie's avatar. "Could she be Black? Or Chinese?"

"Wouldn't that be cultural appropriation? After all, I'd be a white woman embedded behind a Black woman's eyes, looking out from a Black body as if it were my own."

"Who would know? It's not like anyone interacting with you will see you through your avatar's eyes."

"I wonder if the creators of this multi-universe have given that a thought? I mean, how many impersonations could be taking place in the metaverse, with whites pretending to be Blacks, men pretending to be women, children pretending to be adults?"

"Like they already do on Facebook and dating sites? And in Shakespeare? I thought that was the whole point of the metaverse, a place where you could hide out and pretend to be what you were not."

"Maybe," Bertie conceded, "but I still don't like it. I don't want to do it."

"Bertie's right," Daru agreed. "I can't say I'd be amused if she made her online persona an Indian, although I suppose it could be a learning experience to see and feel what it is like when others respond to you as an Indian."

But Bertie had had enough experience of people responding to her as a Jewish other. She didn't need to try out all the other varieties of diversity.

"Can't I just be what I was in 1974 at Venice Beach, a young white woman in her twenties?"

"Then how about a big butt and big tits?" Marion pushed her.

Bertie had never possessed either. To be honest, she had sometimes wished to have been better endowed. It seemed strange to have an avatar so different from her, but the idea appealed. Given her imagined measurements, and Marion's further insistence that both butt and tits should stand high, she now had to think about her wardrobe. What clothes would suit her? Should she wear tight denims, or would looser, thinner material reveal her curves better?

"She should definitely have straight blonde hair cut bluntly just below the shoulders and with thick bangs," Daru contributed.

Bertie had seen pictures of Daru as a child in India, her shiny hair like a sheet of black silk down her back. Now she wore it pulled back in an elegant bun tied with a black ribbon. She was still a pert, attractive woman, ten years younger than Marion and her. Not everyone could be Jane Fonda, but Daru came close with her shapely legs and firm bearing. She had retired early from her TV news announcer job when her bosses suggested she might benefit from a Botox treatment. "Just a little bit," they said, "to get rid of those messy wrinkles around your mouth."

Years after Daru had stormed out KITO's door, her anger still curdled every time she mentioned the communications company. "I suffered for every one of my wrinkles," she told them, pointing at her cheeks where a few lines creased her otherwise smooth brown skin. "This wrinkle I earned bringing up a rambunctious child; this one from being a foreign correspondent in Afghanistan; and this one...that's from when Aditya got cancer."

Had she been darker, of course, her wrinkles would not have shown, but Daru's family, if not exactly Brahmin, had roots in one of the higher castes. Her pale skin lightened even further by years spent in sunless Seattle creased as much as Bertie's. Imagining her telling KITO where to shove their Botox always made her friends laugh. Certainly, nobody could call her a pushover, but of the three of them, she was the one least likely to argue or protest. The charm genes had chosen her, so it seemed she was always saying the right thing and putting people at ease. It drove Marion crazy, and she would often try to goad Daru into passing a mean remark.

"You're too nice, Daru. People will take advantage of you," she warned.

But Daru did not possess a mean streak; she was genuinely kind. Once, when a twisted ankle laid Bertie up, every night she brought her trays of Indian food that perfumed her apartment with turmeric, cumin, and ginger. Everyone adored Daru; what was there to dislike? Sometimes, though, Arielle would go on and on about Daru's emotional generosity, which Bertie thought was taking it a bit too far. What? Had she not given her maternal everything to Arielle when she was growing up?

Since Alex first brought the metaverse to Bertie's attention, she saw information about it everywhere she looked. It was like being pregnant and suddenly the whole world appeared knocked up and every newspaper carried ads about baby clothes and toys. Surprisingly, Daru had never heard of the metaverse during her time at KITO, even though she had been surrounded by young people who kept her on her toes. Dungeons and Dragons, yes, but that was when a lot of people believed the tabletop game had ties to satanism and, fearing for their children's mental and moral health, sent them to rehab. Daru recalled that her son, the architect, sometimes used 3D simulations in his architectural drawings. Being able to see virtually how a building would look when erected revolutionized the way his company did architecture.

Marion, however, still thought Bertie crazy, chasing after something so peripheral to her present life. She kept asking what Bertie hoped to find in this digital world.

"Truth," Daru suggested.

"Hah!" Marion scoffed. The very word raised her freckled hackles.

"I mean *her* truth," Daru tried to explain. "You know, sort of like her own verse in the metaverse."

Bertie turned on her side to face them, her hip hurting with the effort, and wondered what possible truth she might find. The one Daru called the Real, with a capital R, the Phallus of that French philosopher she so loved? Herself?

"I don't know," she said, "I just don't want to be left behind. That's it. Period."

"What?" Marion asked Bertie to repeat herself. She was growing increasingly deaf, but refused to admit it, claiming that Bertie and Daru spoke unclearly. "Stop slurring your words! And don't think I can't see you exchanging amused smiles." She pointed a finger at them. "You two are the problem, not me."

"The world's marching into a new age, Marion, and I don't want to be left behind. I don't want to be on the outside, sitting on the margins of groups, not knowing what on earth their words mean. It would be like deafness of a different kind. You could hear the words alright, but they would be meaningless."

"Like listening to a football commentary," Marion suggested, "or a discussion on catalytic converters? I hate to disillusion you two, but we are already there. When was the last time you completed the *Times* crossword? Do you know the latest singers and social stars who appear as clues? At first, I could work out their names by default through surrounding words. Now, even these ask for cultural icons, and not ones from the seventies either."

"C'mon, guys," Daru interrupted, and sat up. "Let's not get into depressing talk. I think this is all quite exciting. Who knows where it will lead Bertie. At the very least, it will add something different to her life. And if that something turns out to be good, well then, Marion and I will join you."

"And if it's bad?" Bertie asked.

"If it's bad, you are on your own, Old Bean," Marion cackled, then leaned over and gave her one of her bear hugs.

She had once overheard Lennie call her "Old Bean" and thought it insulting until Bertie told her it was an expression of affection, a British one, which she delightedly adopted, though its meaning for Bertie had died along with Lennie.

Yes, Lennie was Canadian, but there were certain inherited English expressions the Canucks guarded jealously. What other words, Bertie thought, could describe that combination of friendship and love she and Lennie sometimes shared? Sure, she wasn't fool enough to expect life to be like that always. There were times when the balance lay entirely on one side leaving the other starved for attention, times when she could quite easily have walked out and advised him to get a dog. Who doesn't need a wake-up call occasionally? What couple doesn't need to recalibrate their balance from time to time?

Was that not why nights out and vacations were invented in the first place?

"Whether your metaverse experiment turns out to be good or bad," Daru persisted, getting back to the nitty-gritty of her avatar, "you still need to name her, Bertie. You can't have this stunning blonde parading along Venice Beach nameless. What is she, twenty-seven? So, born in '47, like you, an early boomer."

"Yup. Along with millions of Anns, Lindas, Carolines, Marilyns, and Sandras." Having had a difficult enough time naming her baby dragon in *Lost Ark*, she had no idea what to call her avatar.

"Look, it really is important to give her a good name if you want her to succeed."

"C'mon, Daru, you don't still believe that stuff." Though Daru had lived in the US most of her life, having come from Uttar Pradesh with her parents as a child of ten, she still held to some traditional Hindu customs.

"Yes. You must give a child a name that expresses your aspirations for it. Take 'Daru,' for example. It means 'cedar' and look which part of America I ended up in!"

"OK, but whatever we name the avatar, she will eventually grow into the name anyway."

They moved into a sort of circle now, Bertie with her legs crossed and Marion and Daru sitting on the edge of their loungers facing her. They came up with some popular names—Rain, Skye, Willow—the nature generation, the very ones most likely to feel the deleterious effects of climate change. Then there were the earlier names like Samantha, Makenzie, and Madison, each of which had its own appeal. Some of the older ones, however, felt more comfortable to Bertie, the stalwarts that had survived generations of baby fashions, names like Julie, Olivia, Rachel, Sarah, Sophie. But they finally settled on Vivienne for Bertie's virtual self, Vivienne meaning "life." Lennie, lover of words, would have appreciated the irony of it.

Vivienne, Bertie now realized, would be everything she was not: long-legged, blue-eyed, and in terms of weight, right smack in that desirable area of being sensually fleshy, but slim. Even her ears would be sexy, like small shells, not long-lobed like hers from wearing heavy, chunky jewelry in her youth.

"You guys have made her into a bimbo!"

She shifted her weight and uncrossed her legs, one of which had pins and needles from having its blood flow restricted. To get the blood moving again, she stood up and shook the affected leg. At least it wasn't a cramp.

"Being a bimbo will be more fun for you," Marion insisted.

"Besides," Daru added, "her external appearance can be a door opener, a way to make connections fast. You, however, will be responsible for what comes out of her mouth. In the end, that's what will decide her personality."

In the games she played with Lisa, Bertie's avatars had been orks, elves, or some other fantastical creatures, but she hadn't yet designed a woman and chosen her nose, her smile, and the highlights in her hair.

The next day when she gave Alex Vivienne's details and read aloud her statistics, he raised an eyebrow. "Whoa!"

"Did you expect something different?"

"I don't know. Maybe. Is Vivienne really what you want?"

She felt embarrassed in front of her son-in-law, wondering what kind of avatar he had envisaged for her. An old lady in sandals and socks picking up shells at the seaside? What fun would that be?

"I thought it would be interesting, you know, different, to put someone sexy like that out in the metaverse. Just to see what happens."

"Suppose so," he answered diffidently.

What did he know about the metaverse that she didn't? Was he imagining something beyond what she in her ignorance could? She watched him fold the piece of paper where she had written Vivienne's measurements and details and hide it in his back pocket.

"I'll get working on her." He cleared his throat. "I mean, I'll model her and write the code for her behaviors."

Bertie could swear he blushed.

# CHAPTER 6

———

DECEMBER ARRIVED AMID FREEZING SNOW AND LAST-minute shopping. Kick-starting the month for Bertie, Lisa's school held its Christmas concert in their auditorium on the ground floor of one of the office blocks that crowded South Lake Union. Although the school emphasized the humanities, it recruited most of its student body from the techie parents who worked in the vicinity. Google, Meta, Microsoft...they all sent their little heirs to be immersed in history and literature, subjects that could not be bound by ones and zeros. It made her wonder what they knew that they weren't sharing with everyone else. Lisa hadn't been permitted to touch a screen until she turned nine.

Bertie was not surprised when she arrived at the school wearing her mask to see private armed guards standing outside the gates. They were there every day, a reminder of the mass shootings that could shatter the peace in a moment of insanity. The children took their presence for granted, but for her, thankful as she was for their protection, it still seemed incongruous that schoolchildren should need to be shielded not just from deranged outsiders but from one of their own. Even in King County, where little tolerance for any kind of gun use existed, disgruntled kids carrying beefs against their classmates could lay their hands on assault weapons.

On stage, the band members settled in their seats. The kids looked so young and innocent. Could any one of them pick up an Uzi and out of anger, depression, or loneliness, cold-bloodedly strafe their classmates? Her eyes slid from one face to the next, looking for signs of...what? She had no idea. She asked Arielle to identify Jared, the bully. He was not in the band, her daughter informed her.

In the rhythm section, a drummer nervously pumped air with his foot pedal and sheepishly acknowledged his parents' waves from the audience. Meanwhile, the brass caressed their highly polished instruments like lovers, one member wiping his sweaty hands from time to time down the side of his pants. Lisa, standing in the middle of the woodwinds, banged her clarinet like a baton against her leg to "de-spit" it. A general chattering hum pervaded the stage.

Like other families in the audience, Arielle, Alex, and Bertie fixed their eyes on their kith and kin.

"Can you hear how Lisa's clarinet tones stand out?" Bertie whispered to Arielle.

Her daughter smiled in agreement, though Bertie doubted she could hear the notes as she did. Jazz had never been Arielle's thing. As a teenager, she had been a hip-hop enthusiast, much to the chagrin of Lennie who did not recognize hip-hop as music, even if he reluctantly admitted when she pointed it out that some of the lyrics were indeed poetic.

"And don't you think her notes are much cleaner and crisper than the other musicians?" Bertie persisted in praising Lisa, despite her daughter patting her arm as if to say, I know, I know, but enough already. "And her transitions, listen to how smooth they sound."

When Lisa stepped out in front of the band to play a solo clarinet version of Benny Goodman's "Moonglow," she grabbed Arielle's hand. Lisa hadn't even told them she had a solo.

Up there on the stage with her eyes closed, Lisa seemed so grown up. Even in the band's uniform of khakis and white T-shirts, the subtle movement of her shoulders revealed she was feeling the unsung words, palpating them with sound, as if she understood love in some instinctive way in her gut. Her bandmaster surely had not taught her to play with her body as well as her mouth. No, this performance was all Lisa.

When Lennie still lived, Lisa would sometimes accompany him to jazz festivals despite Bertie's hesitations about her being too young. How could he expect an 8-year-old to sit still, she'd objected; she would get bored and disturb everyone in the audience. But Lisa had proved her wrong. Perched there alongside her grandfather, breathing in the music, and feeling its tremulous vibrato in her body, she had listened to the music, totally enthralled. Afterward, back home, she would surprise them with her new vocabulary learned at his side: cadence, double time, and jam, not of the strawberry variety.

Now, as she neared the end of "Moonglow," she moved smoothly through the melodic riff. With steady fingers pressing on the pads, she bounced and swayed as if the music danced inside her. When finally, she swooped her clarinet up, her long hair fell back, and the last precious notes—*Moonglow gave me you*—sprang free. She had paid tribute in her own unique way to the King of Swing.

Afterward, when she took her bow and everyone stood up to applaud an exceptional performance, Bertie turned to the neighbors behind her and beaming from ear to ear kvelled:

"That's my granddaughter up there!"

●●

It was "Moonglow" that gave her Lennie in 1975.

She never quite knew what Lennie saw in her. They met in 1974 soon after her and Christine's vacation at Venice Beach. Whereas she had been fleeing a broken marriage at the time, Christine had been engaged to a lovely young man and was simply taking a breather before plunging into the marital depths. In the two weeks they enjoyed their freedom, Christine never considered a last fling, though she certainly felt flattered by the attention men paid her, which perhaps confirmed for her she was not merely drifting into a comfortable, ongoing relationship, but actively making a choice to marry. Within weeks of returning to her fiancé in Vancouver, Canada, she announced their wedding date.

As her bridesmaid, Bertie had several duties to fulfill during the ceremony, but these did not stop her from noticing one of the guests, Leonard Glazer. At the time, Lennie worked as a journalist for the *Vancouver Sun*. Not yet the syndicated columnist he would later become, nor the governor's press officer whose name everyone knew, he nevertheless commanded attention. She had noticed him immediately—most of the women had—but she thought he was surely out of her league romantically. He stood to one side of the room discussing the fall of Saigon with a group of young American men who did not take kindly to advice from a Canadian who hadn't fled his country to escape the draft. In his dark suit and tie—dashikis and sandals were passé by 1974—he looked taller than her, an added attraction since she measured 5 feet 11 in her bare feet. His hair he still wore long in the neck.

The Rumble in the Jungle boxing match between George Foreman and Muhammad Ali in Kinshasa, Zaire, seemed to be on everyone's lips. Since she had nothing to contribute to a boxing conversation and had exhausted her discussion on Nixon's resignation to avoid impeachment, she tried her luck with this new fellow. She had never been able to resist a good political argument, so, accepting her romantic limitations with him, she edged closer to find out what he had to say about Vietnam. From where she stood, she could hear him parry arguments without raising his voice or losing his cool. He held a glass of red wine in his right hand and occasionally he would sip from it as if to give his listeners time to ponder his last point. When somebody brought up the casualties and the cost in American lives, she joined his circle—what was there to lose—and waded into the fray. Though usually her arguments were more bluster than rhetoric, she was on firm ground with this one having direct experience with the fallout from the war. Hadn't she personally tended to the wounds of mangled and destroyed bodies at West Roxbury? Hadn't she held sobbing young men in her arms, offering paltry words of encouragement which she knew could never override the horror lodged in their hearts?

Leonard Glazer was not immune to her passion. Yes, how terrible the losses, he agreed, and what a waste of young lives. He quoted the numbers of Americans dead—over 58,000—and injured—over 153,00—and missing in action—almost 2,000—but soon returned to his effortless logic, stressing what she realized was as important to him as the deaths, namely, how the war had ripped apart the social fabric when poor families realized how many sons of the wealthy had escaped the carnage. That was where his interest lay, in the American unfairness of it all. War was inevitable given the Communist hysteria of the time.

Bertie could not make him out. Was he a Communist sympathizer? A Conservative pro-war supporter? Did he imply that Canada would not have done the same? She kept asking him questions, trying to place him in one of the boxes that sorted people into manageable lots. In her head, other boxes made of ticky-tacky were still being unloaded from the bowels of military planes. Even so, she found herself losing sight of her side of the argument. Lennie had an unsettling way when he talked to someone of locking eyes, assuring the person of his full attention. When the thumping beat of "Midnight Special" distracted her and her gaze skittered sideways to the happy dancers letting it all hang out, as people used to say then, he touched her arm and brought her attention back. In those days, she never stopped wanting to know more, always peppering her conversation with what, why, and how. She wasn't trying to corner Lennie's attention; the questioning was just her normal way of being. So, explain to me, she would say. Thinking back on it now, perhaps that was why he fell for her: she wanted to know, and he wanted to tell.

The other Americans had drifted away, and it was just her and him. The music had changed to slower numbers, and they had slowed down, their talk having covered huge swaths of material. This was as good a time as any to move on. She wanted to speak to the bride, anyway. But Lennie had other ideas. He took her by the arm and led her onto the dance floor. He never asked if she wanted to dance. He just gave her that amused smile that dimpled his cheek.

"Moonglow" played.

Less than two years later, they celebrated their wedding, and she moved to Vancouver to start her new life as Mrs. Glazer.

●●

"How do you know when you are in love, Gran?"

Lisa's question brought her to a sudden halt. They were in the middle of Pike Street Market checking out the booths where long-time vendors sold shiny apples and, if you weren't paying attention, substituted a less spectacular sample from under the table. A group of tourists coming up from behind had been looking backward over their shoulders at Malcolm, the fishmonger, slinging a silvery salmon to his colleague Bob, and they now walked straight bang into Bertie. While apologizing to them profusely, she gathered her wits about her for Lisa. At seventy-five, what did falling in love mean? And what did it mean at thirteen?

"Not that I'm ever planning to fall in love. I mean it makes people so dorky you want to puke." She rifled through a pack of different colored T-shirts that read "meh!" then told her about Gina, a girl in her class who fell in love regularly every month. "You would think she'd been scoffing magic mushrooms by the hundreds. Really! She looks dazed. You can't even get a sensible word out of her. And then—even worse—when the love affairs fall apart, she collapses into a sobbing snotball in the bathroom."

Christmas shoppers milled around them, stopping now and then to handle a tooled leather belt or to sniff at hand lotion smelling of lavender and promising "no artificial ingredients." A carver displayed his wooden xylophones, then took up a couple of soft-headed mallets to pound at the notes so they could hear the exactitude of their tones. Above the sound, Christmas singers caroled over loudspeakers about holly and jingle bells and good King Wenceslas, while on the street buskers hoping to earn a few dollars rapped about being homeless in Amazonia. Nobody sang about love, not even of the kind reserved for God. Caesar and God each knew his place, and this market smelling of roasted coffee, spices, piroshki, and hot cider was commercial territory.

"Most people don't really know for sure they are in love," she said cautiously, trying to feel her way, "because it's so easy to confuse these kinds of magic mushroom feelings with...well, other things. But it's a good feeling either way, even if it does make you look dorky."

She glanced at Lisa. Had she heard her? Bent over a flower vendor's counter, she sniffed at greenhouse azaleas and begonias. She ran her fingers over the furry pussy willows the vendors added to their bouquets for texture. Bertie recalled several love limericks of her favorite rock songs, but nothing appropriate came back, at least nothing that would make sense to Lisa. Strangely enough, she had known when she fell in love with Lennie. About a year after their dance to "Moonglow," when they had passed the initial stage of mutual attraction and lust, they had visited his parents' home where they had slept together in his childhood bed surrounded not by balsa-wood airplanes or Tonka trucks, but by lifelike metal sculptures, not over three inches high he had made from thick bent wires. A ballet dancer, a skater, a drunkard, and a woodcutter stood among the figurines that watched over them from the top of the bookcase. Their funny, skinny bodies and twirled wire hair elicited an affection in her that made her look at Lennie differently, for they spoke to something beyond the wordsman she had grown to know and whom she suspected sometimes concealed himself behind his armor of words. Here in the room of his childhood, she fell in love. Who can say why? Who knows what odd or ordinary things suddenly assume meaning.

"Do you think Emory would like this for Hanukkah?" Lisa held up a sequin-covered book bag that could barely hold two books. Bertie already knew Emory from Lisa's school; he was her best friend; she could quite easily imagine him wearing the bag.

"But getting back to love," Bertie began, giving Rachel the brass pig a pat on her rump as they passed. Was Lisa having feelings for this boy who sometimes came over to the apartment to play online games?

"Wait," she said, pulling out a stick of gum and chewing it furiously. "Let's go stick this up on the Gum Wall."

To hell with love. And off they went.

# CHAPTER 7

———

THE FOUNDER OF THE COLLAPSED CRYPTOCURRENCY exchange, FTX, filled the newspapers' headlines. Authorities indicted him of wire fraud and money laundering, causing rich young people to have second thoughts about the security of their crypto dealings. What would that mean for the metaverse? she wondered. If players could not make online purchases of clothes, furniture, and land, would the entire structure come tumbling down? After all, without the financial underpinnings of this new invisible entity, what was the point for many investors?

At this stage, the whole idea of the metaverse for Bertie was just that, an idea, so it was easy to think of it in the abstract. Alex still prepared her little realm, so she had yet to experience how it would bring her to a more intimate identification with its workings. As a topic, however, something she might discuss at a cocktail party if she ever went to one, she could look at it from different angles and identify its potential problems, about which Marion, in her Cassandra voice, had already warned her.

Yes, the sociological pressures on young girls like Lisa might be even worse in the metaverse than they already were on TikTok and Instagram, heaven forbid, and yes, there was nothing to stop right-wing groups from doing whatever they wanted in their own realms if they hid beyond the reach of left-wing spoilers. They already did that plenty. Also, harassment and revenge porn, a huge problem on the internet, could be even worse. Then there was the question of the Digital Divide: Who could afford to interact in this brave new world? Already, the games she enjoyed with Lisa allowed players to pay to progress up the ladder more quickly to a max level where they could engage in more challenging content. It was stuff players could brag about.

When she spoke to Alex, he assured her the tech companies were aware of her questions and control mechanism protection for developers like himself were already in place. Everyone was taking a chance, including him, trusting in the ability of great minds to work things out as they developed. Bertie visualized this huge invisible edifice balanced on thousands of upstretched hands. *The King is in the altogether...*Yet, who could deny the excitement of the whole thing, the myriad possibilities that were leaping ecstatically from pipe dreams? It felt like they were on the verge of something that might revolutionize the way people lived. Good? Bad? She didn't know, but there were a lot of minds hurtling headfirst into it. Were it not for Lisa's games that gave Bertie entry into these worlds, she would not even have imagined such possibilities. When she thought of the various game worlds she had entered, each one more sophisticated than the next, she felt grateful to her granddaughter for having introduced her to them, and to her doctor for encouraging her to stay.

As it happened, she and Lisa hadn't played any games for a week or two. The Christmas break was a busy time, and other than on Christmas day when the whole family got together to eat and exchange gifts, she didn't see Lisa. She had parties to attend, movies to watch, and friends to visit. Bertie, however, felt the need to start the New Year with a bang. So, she dragged Daru and Marion, shouting and protesting, to the shores of Lake Washington for the annual Polar Plunge. There, at Madison Beach, where an assortment of twenty to thirty other shivering bathers huddled under their beach towels to stay warm, they curled their toes into the sodden sand and prepared themselves for the shock of entering this wet meta-world.

Storm clouds gathered above, and the temperature read thirty-seven degrees Fahrenheit. With chattering teeth and goose-bumped flesh, the intrepid bathers waited for someone to blow the whistle and send them charging into the frigid water.

"You know we're risking cardiac arrest," Marion moaned, rubbing her arms to create friction.

And then, they were in, thrashing and screaming like they always did, quickly dunking themselves to their necks in the belief the water would be warmer than the air.

"I don't know why I let you push me into doing this." Daru lobtailed the water surface like an orca, slapping it with her arm and spraying Bertie in revenge.

Wet strands of hair hung like seaweed on her neck; sea spray stuck between Bertie's eyelashes. Marion, not wanting to be left out of the action, splashed a wave in their direction, causing her and Daru to stampede from the lake, feet stumbling painfully over the pebbles, breath coming in short, sharp puffs. Desperately they pulled their dry clothes over wet skin, collecting lumps of sand in their sweatsuit pants. Every follicle on their bodies stood to attention, hearts thumping, and back teeth aching. In each cell, a vibrato resonated and made strange music with the nonsensical sounds emanating from their flapping jaws and uncontrollable lips. The body could not be denied; the body was real, even old bodies. No one could say they were invisible.

That night, invigorated as they were from their plunge, they joined the other inhabitants of Mariela Plaza in a New Year celebration. The affair took place on the top floor of their building in the special party room that looked out onto shimmering city lights, but only on one side. At the other end of the room, where one would expect to see twinkling stars over the Sound, no light penetrated. For the occasion, they had dressed up as best they could though most young people, except for Phillip and David who appeared in matching velvet suits, came more casually clad in jeans.

At Marion's instigation, Bertie had straightened her hair and twisted it into a loosely wound ponytail/bun that stuck out on the sides as if she had put it up in a hurry, when in fact it had taken her forty minutes to get the look right. Why she bothered, she didn't know. She even darkened her eyelashes with mascara, like Daru did hers with kohl. But ha! There was still no "sea-change into something rich and strange."

When they entered the room, they were greeted by a handful of children running around the huge space, chasing one another with wooden skewers and discarding shrimps, onions, and green peppers underfoot. Since the three of them knew very few of their neighbors—most disappeared off to work in the morning and came back late at night—they were determined to circulate and widen their horizons. Other people's lives always fascinated Bertie. Enriched her even. She was certain some of their neighbors had intriguing tales to share and she was eager to find out more. But, though she, Daru, and Marion each tried to start conversations, querying several strangers about their work and their interests, their exchanges never went anywhere. Or at least, nobody picked up on comments they made and followed through, asking in turn about their lives and interests. Shouldn't they at least have been curious about which floor

Bertie lived on, if not what she had done before retiring, or whether she had grandchildren? Well, it was their loss, Bertie thought, for she had so much more to offer now than she had in her twenties. Damn it, she had wisdom, hadn't she! Isn't that what people said about oldsters? As late-life lovies, they had wisdom to pass down, but nobody wanted their wisdom.

Perhaps Nancy Pelosi, Ruth Bader Ginsburg, and Hillary Clinton could have played the room better, but she, Daru, and Marion were women who had retired from ordinary jobs, great jobs even, but ones that did not make them instantly recognizable or, in Daru's case, no longer familiar.

Then there was this, as Marion put it bluntly: "Why would people want to talk to an old biddy with no job, introductions, or connections to offer?"

"Stop kvetching," Daru scolded Marion. Over the years, she had picked up the odd Yiddish word from the two of them. "You have to keep an open mind. And anyway, who are you calling an old lady?" she tut-tutted and, smoothing her eyebrows, moved in on another small group, this one a knot of 40-year-olds engrossed in conversation. Even as she did so, Marion argued that without recognition from years in the public arena, even Pelosi and Clinton would struggle to break into the small cliques standing around them at the party. Try seeing those politicians without their trappings, and they'd be just two old ladies with lots of wrinkles.

Meanwhile, Daru stood on the edge of the new group, mouthing her name in greeting. Though she received the odd smile and nod, nobody seemed to recognize her from her KITO days. In any case, the five men and women were too deeply involved in their discussion to stop and include her, so she ended up on the margins of their circle, sipping her glass of sauvignon blanc. Had they been talking about anything other than the West Point treatment plant opposite Discovery Park, she could have contributed insightful information. No fool, Daru, she was well-read and kept up with new ideas. About sewerage, however, she drew a blank. To save her, Bertie and Marion linked arms and whisked her away from the group, loudly speaking of the TV producer they wanted her to meet.

"You know…what's his name again?" Bertie said, debriding Daru's wound.

They ended up talking not to a TV producer but to one of Marion's ex-dates, Matthew, a 75-year-old ex-banker, who proved no fun at all, since she had recently turned down his invitation to a weekend at his cabin at Cannon Beach and he appeared in no mood to play nice. He did, however, introduce them to two young women, Janet and Lindiwe, clay artists each with her own design style, who invited them to visit their studios in the SODO area, near the stadium. Ironic though it might be, they too preferred talking to young people rather than old. Their conversation invigorated the Golden Girls, made them feel that maybe they should take pottery lessons. It should have made them more understanding given their own aged situations, but they weren't that generous. In any case, as the evening progressed, they had fun despite it all.

"You know," Bertie said, as they rode the elevator down to their apartments, "there are some advantages to being invisible."

Marion gave her a skeptical look and said, "Name just one."

"Well, people pay more attention to what you're saying if they aren't also ogling you at the same time."

"Yeah, but you have to get them to want to talk to you in the first place," Marion countered, reminding them of their invisible status earlier.

"Also," Daru said, supporting Bertie, "when you're invisible, you don't have to put up with colleagues making lurid remarks when all you want to talk to them about is statistical analyses."

"And I suppose if you happened to be in a store during a holdup, it is unlikely you would be chosen as a hostage," Marion mocked them.

"It's not all about men, you know. Young women also don't see us," Bertie argued, essentially ceding Marion the point. "Sometimes they are worse than males and will walk right over you if you don't get out of the way."

"Not surprising," she said. "After all, you are what they hope never to be."

● ●

The next day, Bertie gave Marion a ride to the airport. None of their trio enjoyed driving at night, but Marion's cataracts must have been worse than hers since Bertie could ignore the halos that radiated around the lights of oncoming cars. Off to London to visit her two daughters, Megan and Laura, and celebrate Laura's fiftieth birthday, Marion looked anxious.

"Are you quite sure you can see?"

Bertie promised to pick her up on January 5 because traveling wasn't so much fun anymore and after a cross-ocean trip, even having to roll your suitcase into the garage to pick up an Uber ride could be the hair that broke the camel's back. Marion already had back problems.

She also had migraine problems. Last week, for whatever reason, she came down with a bad attack. Perhaps the realization that she now had a daughter of half a century paralyzed her brain cells, but she took to her bed. As always, she switched off the lights and lay there in the dark with a hot compress on her head. Bertie brought her a bowl of her chicken soup which Marion claimed remained the only food she could stomach in her state. She called it her magic potion. So frequent were

Marion's migraines that Bertie kept a permanent supply of her magic potion frozen.

So, between one thing and another, she had been busy, and it wasn't until the first day of school that Lisa and she reconnected. Around her neck Bertie had wound the soft cashmere scarf Lisa had knitted as a present for her and when she opened the door, her granddaughter curled herself into it so the two of them got tangled up together.

"Listen," Bertie said, twirling her out in a Twist dance move. If she had been wearing one of those sixties skirts with layers of petticoats, they would have floated up and swirled around her. "Your dad has persuaded his pals at Sarssein to let me participate in the user-research study from home, instead of going into their offices in person. I don't know how he did it, but he told them a sob story about my age and the dangers of Covid if I had to traipse into the building every day, and so they made an exception. Which means—ta-da—I will have the VR headset at the apartment to use whenever I want."

"That's great, Gran!"

"So, now, I need your help. Before my new metaverse becomes ready for occupation, we need to choose the music that will make it feel real."

"Well, what kind of music? I know what you and Gramps used to listen to," she said, helping herself to a raisin bagel and slurping orange juice direct from the bottle. "But what did you like in 1974? Were you into folk music like Peter, Paul and Mary stuff?"

What Bertie sought in music then was to be transported. Get her away from the blood and guts of her everyday wards to the escapist fantasies of the pop world. Like Lisa, she had always responded to music viscerally, jumping up at the first bar to move her body whichever way the music pulled. She couldn't sit still. Even when alone, her body answered as if the earth itself called it out to play.

As soon as Lisa had settled herself at Bertie's computer and checked her phone—Arielle texted often, just to be in touch—she pulled up YouTube and scrolled through lists of classic hits from the sixties and seventies.

"My favorite, you already know, is CCR."

But there were also Jefferson Airplane, the Rolling Stones, Fleetwood Mac, Aerosmith, the Eagles, and even the Beach Boys, about whom Lennie was often less than flattering. Although Bertie learned to love Lennie's jazz and gradually moved in that direction, she never gave up on her first loves.

"And what about the Beatles?"

"Of course!"

"Well, let's start putting together a playlist and when I get home, I will give it to my dad to incorporate in your metaverse." Lisa was organized, like her mother. "So, then, what are your favorite cuts from each group?"

"From each group? Don't I only need about four tunes in total?"

She didn't expect to spend more than a couple of sessions in her new realm; just enough time to find out what it was all about so she could satisfy her curiosity and give Alex and Sarssein some feedback about the crazy unreal world he and other young men of his ilk were creating in competition with one another. Who would get the finished product to the market first? That was what drove them. Meta already had Oculus out there, Google its augmented reality glasses, and Snap its Spectacles headset, Alex had told her. Although she had inched forward in her general, abstract understanding of virtual reality, his words still meant little to her on the ground. How were augmented reality glasses, which Alex called AR, different from

VR? Until she actually placed the damn VR headset on her head, she had no idea. She was swimming upstream through a river of acronyms with no salmon ladder to help her on her way. Incomprehensible words still washed over and through her.

"Of course you will need lots of music," Lisa assured her. "You don't want to listen to the same cuts over and over again. I mean, if it's really lit in your realm and you love it, you will want to spend more time there."

"Not likely," she replied, making herself comfy on Lennie's favorite chair and slipping off her shoes.

She could still only imagine her metaverse like one of the games she played with Lisa, albeit in the context of Venice Beach. The possibility of spending hours in such an environment seemed unlikely, since she hardly ever passed more than thirty minutes on the games she entered with her granddaughter before her head started throbbing. All those flashing lights, speed, and people whizzing by...But then, her granddaughter knew more about virtual reality than she did, so she went along with her anyway.

"OK, let's do it," she said and suggested the Stones' "Jumpin' Jack Flash" video.

Lisa had never heard the song, or if she had, it had been background noise to which she had not paid attention. Now, listening carefully to the Stones, she admitted they weren't so bad at all.

"Good beat," she conceded before giggling, "but that hair... and that mouth!"

Mick's rubber lips in the video contorted just like Bertie remembered them, seeming to reshape the words as he spewed them out. How young and thin they all were then, innocent even, in the sense of simply standing up there on the stage playing their music without the spectacle or glitter they adopted for their performances later. The music was the thing; that was what audiences came for; to feel alive. Her body's memory responded now to the beat, as if fifty years hadn't intervened. She could still see herself dancing barefoot to "Jumpin' Jack Flash" in a long rainbow-colored skirt, a bandana tied across her forehead.

"But what was the 'Hotel California,' Gran?" And then, "Who or what was 'Proud Mary'?"

Even as she asked her about the songs, Lisa bounced on the computer chair; she was keeping on rollin', as CCR said. Soon, her feet in their big boots were tapping to "My Generation," just as Bertie had in her twenties. She and her friends, now in their seventies, had screamed along with The Who, telling the older generation to get lost, to just fade away. They were ready to run the world, and they would run it better. By the time "Midnight Special" boomed out, Bertie was already on her feet.

"Turn it up, Lisa," she encouraged her and felt the music bouncing off the floor and walls.

There was something about this CCR hit that always got her up dancing. Moving in her old-fashioned style that was perfectly attuned to the music's beat, if not her knees, she held out her hand to Lisa.

"C'mon," she said, pulling her up.

"Nah, I don't know how to dance to this kind of music. Besides, you look ridiculous!"

"I know," Bertie said, accentuating her movements, knowing her hips would suffer for it later, "but I am having such fun. And look, you are already dancing in your seat, and anyway, no matter how you dance, you can't look more ridiculous than me, sweetheart."

Lisa giggled and stood up tentatively.

"Go for it," Bertie said, and Lisa jutted out her elbows and waved her arms trying to adapt her Z-generation dance moves to the beat.

Bertie already sang at full throttle and, though Lisa did not know the words, she joined in on the chorus, both of them belting out their enthusiasm for the midnight special train that could carry you far away from your troubles. She sometimes wondered whether the singer wanted the train to slam straight into him, like a bullet from that other "midnight special."

"What the hell?" And there was Daru standing at the open door, mouth agape.

They hadn't heard her knock, so she let herself in. They each had keys to all three apartments so they could check that one of them wasn't lying on the floor pathetically shouting, "Help me, I've fallen, and I can't get up." Although Bertie waved to Daru, she made no move to stop what she was doing. While the music still played, she and Lisa had no intention of interrupting that feeling of being totally in sync rhythmically with the other, so they continued to dance and sing, Bertie an octave lower than her granddaughter, she, spilling it out as if she had found the exact accompaniment to whatever lay bottled up in her teenage mind.

Daru, not to be outdone, kicked off her fashionable heels and ignoring the arthritis in her left leg, moved in on their little dance party and shone her own spontaneous light on it. With her stylized Indian hand movements, together with Lisa's elbowing and her shoulder pumping—her shoulders were the only part of her that didn't hurt—they created a strange tableau.

When the music finally ended, the three of them stood as in a rugby scrum, exhausted, hanging onto one another, and feeling totally alive.

# CHAPTER 8

THE WEEKS PASSED QUICKLY. IN THE *SEATTLE TIMES*, reports of hundreds of techie workers being let go shocked the community. At first it was Meta, then Microsoft, but eventually Amazon, too, as these companies tried to compensate for their financial losses. For those laid off and locked out of their projects, non-compete clauses made it impossible to accept other jobs in the city, leading many to uproot their families and move to California or Texas. Foreign workers fared even worse, losing their US visas unless they could find a new position within three months.

Alongside these massive layoffs, violent crime went up steadily in King County. Near Arielle's home, automatic live fire kept residents on edge in the early hours of the morning. A gang of crooks stole catalytic converters or simply held up drivers at gunpoint when they stopped their cars at traffic lights. Nobody shouted any longer about defunding the police, no matter how sympathetic to Black Lives Matter grievances, not even those who had initially demanded it. The city needed protection. Although many of the downtown buildings had reopened, in the International District, grocery stores owned by Chinese Americans remained boarded up, their fronts despoiled by racist graffiti. No Harings or Basquiats appeared among the taggers.

Then, at the end of January to commemorate the fifty-first anniversary of *Roe v. Wade*, they joined the Women's March. The number of marchers was down, however, and only the die-hards turned up.

Against this depressing background, Aditya's cancer had advanced to the point where the drugs to control his pain no longer worked and he was admitted to Cancer Care Alliance at Fred Hutch where he died on March 22 under heavy doses of morphine. Daru had been living in expectation of his death for the last couple of years, yet his disappearance from her life came as a shock. She was devastated and kept blaming herself. If only she had pushed him when he refused to get regular colonoscopies, always putting off the test as if he knew something didn't feel right but resisted knowing. Perhaps then, they might have caught the cancer before it spread to his bones. Her only son, Nikel, the architect, flew in from Chicago the night of his death, and the next day Daru had Aditya cremated, according to Hindu custom, that his soul might transition peacefully to his next life. The rest of that Saturday, the two of them, mother and son, dressed in white, sat quietly in the Amazon Spheres surrounded by waterfalls, terrariums, and plants. In that tranquil rain forest, Daru told them afterward, though they tried to remember only happy things about Aditya, in both their minds was his disapproval of Nikel's homosexuality and his disappointment that he would never have grandchildren.

With Nikel at her side for the first four days of the mourning period, Daru held herself together, but once he left, the emptiness of their apartment hit her hard. Where Aditya had always sat at the head of the dining room table, now stood his vacant chair with the cushion that still bore a red stain from the time he choked on his Chateau Ste. Michelle cabernet. His pain had caused him to draw a deep breath, with the resultant gagging and spluttering of wine through mouth and nose. In the basket next to their bed lay his watch and glasses as if just waiting for him to wake up and return them to their normal place. Like Chuck Schumer, Aditya had always worn his glasses at the end of his nose, peering over the top rims when he spoke to you, like the teacher he had once been.

Nine days of *Teravih* remained before the mourning period ended, days that Daru had to get through before normal life could once again begin. Marion and Bertie took turns sitting with her, paging through old photograph albums or listening to stories from the early days of their marriage when Aditya constantly had to prove to her parents that though he came from a slightly lower caste than their daughter, he had succeeded in America and had the means to give Daru everything her heart could desire. Their marriage had turned out to be a happy one.

Just as weddings always brought back images from Bertie's own marriage day, so did death elicit thoughts of her bereavement. Seeing Aditya in the hospital reminded her how awful Lennie's passing had been. The one time she could see him before the hospital closed their doors to visitors, a breathing mask covered his face, and his chest heaved with his desperate effort to stay alive. It had all happened so quickly. Arielle, dealing with Covid among her young patients, had warned them to take every precaution to protect themselves. "Your age makes you extra vulnerable," she'd said. "Get vaccinated and stay home! Have your groceries delivered!" They followed her advice and that of Dr. Fauci, but perhaps they had not waited long enough for the vaccine's protection to kick in before a cavalier Lennie went to listen to a jazz musician playing at a small café in their neighborhood. Within a few days, his throat grew scratchy, and he started to cough. He could not get his breath. Breathe or talk; talk or breathe? Neither lay in his power anymore. He had always been a healthy man, but his heart medications didn't protect him from the strength of this ugly virus's attack. Within the week, he was gone, and all his beautiful, forceful, gentle, romantic words along with him.

Bertie struggled through the two years following Lennie's death, made worse by the isolation of Covid restrictions. Like Daru, she second-guessed herself. Had she done enough to protect Lennie from the virus? Could she have insisted more adamantly on his staying away from public places? She was a nurse, for heaven's sake, with more than fifty years of experience.

Having worn her mask religiously, she avoided catching the bug herself, but in trying to stay alive, she had also died a little. It was hard to say exactly what died or how. Perhaps it was her connection with people, her sense of being in the world with them, empathizing, being one with them, she didn't know. But a little wall had gradually grown around her, and around everyone else, each of them in her own private loneliness, secluded, solitary, protecting their health from "them."

Though she, Daru, and Marion trusted one another to take precautions for the protection of them all, they were still less hands-on than before. No sipping from each other's wineglass, nor taking a peck at the other's food to see what it tasted like, no close hugs. Panic erupted when one of them sneezed too close to the other or coughed. Zooming barely scratched the surface of their aloneness.

During this period, she became Daru and Marion's doctor-on-call, especially in the middle of the night. So many Covid symptoms had been reported that every scratchy throat or upset stomach convinced them their luck had run out. "Is it serious? Should I see someone about it? What medicine can I take to get through the night?" She kept a veritable pharmacy in her bathroom, most of it under lock and key, out of reach of Lisa. None of them wanted to be by herself with an unexplained pain at two in the morning. Being reassured by one another, or even just making voice contact, allowed them to feel not so alone.

Lisa, her portal into the world of the living during this time, went through her own trials and tribulations over loss, the two of them commiserating and seeking escape in the multiverse of gaming.

With the gradual return of better days, she, Daru, and Marion had headed hungrily to the places where they could once again experience the intoxication of noisy crowds. Albeit with masks—none of them wanted to gamble with the few years still allotted to them—they resumed their visits to the symphony, the public market, and their favorite restaurants, ready to grab the world by the ears and once again start living.

●●

"What's it like to be so old, Gran?" Lisa asked her.

They had been listening to another very old person giving the State of the Union address on TV and, to her mind, show-ing a good amount of vigor for his age, especially toward the end when he raised his hands and announced that America was back.

Lisa sat in Lennie's chair with her feet resting on the edge of the glass coffee table, staring out at the Puget Sound through the floor-to-ceiling windows. Drunken gray clouds engorged with liquid scudded across the sky, driven by a stiff breeze that stirred up sudden squalls over the Olympic Mountains that forced the swollen, bulging clouds to release the contents of their bellies.

"Actually, I am fine with being old, sweetheart...as long as I have you."

She gave her an affectionate smile, but Bertie guessed where she was going with her question. She had lost Lennie and now Daru's husband had died. Would her grandmother be next? In the distance outside, Bertie could see container boats fighting their way through the disturbed seas, disappearing in the troughs before rising high again on the waves.

"I know..." Lisa prevaricated, trying to find the right words that wouldn't hurt her gran's feelings or make her sad. "But doesn't it feel sort of weird to know you may only be alive for another five or ten years? It's not very long," she explained. "I mean, I've got another seventy years at least."

"Lucky you! You're just a chick!"

Lisa was too thoughtful a person to feed some bromide or offer a candy-flavored explanation about death. To Bertie's mind, death was one hazard of living, so that was what she told her, adding that each year could be as long as you made it. "If you fill it with life and friendships, a year can seem to go on for ages."

Lisa looked away, self-conscious perhaps about such serious talk. She slipped her feet to the ground, then wiped the smudges they had left on the glass tabletop.

At school, Lisa had a small group of like-minded friends—her squad, she called them—who so far had avoided the attractions of TikTok and Instagram. Holding out despite occasional aspersions on their nerdiness, they created strange, off-key musical compositions and animated comics online. Her closest friend, Emory, was a spunky 13-year-old who still looked ten but whose brain seemed always to be in overdrive.

He wanted to be a physicist, he told Bertie. He had fallen in love with the universe out there and was convinced that they lived multi-lives and on some distant planet, another Emory experienced a very different existence from his own on earth.

"There are probably several Berties out there too, Mrs. Glazer," he assured her. "Maybe one of you is living in another country, or maybe one never even married."

If only you knew, Emory! Soon, another Bertie would indeed be living in someplace else—multiverse, metaverse—and only one of them would be aware of the existence of the other.

Sometimes, Emory would join Lisa at the apartment and play the more complex games with her that Bertie couldn't handle. She would watch them enviously, marveling at the quickness of their brains as well as their fingers, and their ability to attend simultaneously to everything happening on the screen. She hadn't seen Emory since before Christmas, but when he came back from school with Lisa the other day, it was obvious he had experienced a growth spurt. His sweater didn't quite reach his wrists, and he walked self-consciously, as if still adjusting to an extra inch or two of height. She had bought a couple of chocolate croissants from the French bakery downstairs and gave hers to him. He devoured it in seconds, leaving a thin line of chocolate on his upper lip, like a lipstick liner.

When her watch pinged, she went to the kitchen to check her phone.

*Do U want to doorbell our bldg. with me Thurs. eve for Dem. Party?—Marion*

*What does Party want to know?* she texted back, then switched on the kettle.

*The usual—What priority should Party focus on the rest of this year?*

*Can we do it after supper once Alex picks up Lisa?*
*Sure. More likely to find people at home then.*

She and Marion made a good canvassing team. They complemented each other and did better together than each one on her own. It helped their case that their building was a safe blue bet, where even the investment bankers among them voted left/center rather than right. Still, with the surprising success of the midterm election behind them, ordinary Democrats were now sitting back self-satisfied, no longer fearing the end of democracy. Tonight, she and Marion would shake them up a bit, scare them with a series of what ifs. What if the Republican-created electors could overrule the real electors of a state? What if the new gerrymandering deprived Democrats of their usual supporters? What if America went to war with Russia over Ukraine? What if disillusioned Republicans formed a new party?

Not that it was only politics that drove her and Marion to canvass. Their door-to-door appeals also offered a way to undertake social forensics and uncover just who their neighbors were in this thirty-floor building that during the day could seem like a mausoleum. In the penthouse, two colorful celebrities she'd never heard of hid from the paparazzi and played music that sounded like dirges, while a smartly attired drug dealer in 2208 went out at midnight, then slept off something powerful the entirety of the next day. There were few nuclear families living at Mariela Plaza, so one seldom heard crying babies, though there were a bunch of young boys, game players, who all seemed to know one another and went to the same school. For a while, a wealthy Nigerian couple, the man a government minister, she believed, lived on the twelfth floor, and reared two rambunctious little boys who had a field day riding the elevator up and down while calling out the floors in Yoruba. She loved it.

Doorbelling their block was also how Marion had met some of the older men she sometimes dated. While Bertie wasn't averse to having male company now and then, nobody her age made any impression. Neither the Botoxed types smelling of men's cologne nor the ones who let it all hang out: take me as I am. It was one of the hazards of being old, she had long ago realized, that you came belatedly to the other, in that you saw the person as he was at his present age, not knowing the fascinating and attractive man he might have been years ago before you knew him. With aging husbands, it worked in the opposite direction. What you saw in your head most of the time was the man he used to be when youth had given him vigor and beauty. An unexpected glimpse of the old man from a distance sometimes came as a shocking reminder.

●●

When she returned to the living room, she found the two kids with their heads buried inside one of her older photograph albums. Who still owns photo albums these days? She had scanned many of the pictures and had them online, but there was something special about looking at the physical photo with its creases and discolorations, its bent edges speaking of other hands. After Lennie's death, Lisa often paged through the albums, searching for pictures of her grandfather at an earlier age. Her head sang with stories Bertie had told her about their lives in Vancouver and what Lennie had been like then. Tell me again, she would beg. She especially relished hearing about silly things he had done. One time, returning from work, he had slid down the snowy hill to their house on his briefcase, arriving at their gate with an open-armed "Ta-da!" Embarrassing things he said would tickle her too. No, she'd guffaw, did he really say that?

And she would laugh out loud, flashing her Lennie-dimple, and wish she had been there.

This time, however, it wasn't Lennie's photo she poured over. She was showing Emory a picture of Bertie.

"Wow," she heard him say, "your grandmother used to be a hottie."

"Yeah, she was beautiful then. See how long her legs were, even in that weird old-fashioned swimsuit."

Stepping back into the kitchen before they could see her, Bertie wondered what kids their age found beautiful. She certainly had been no stunner then, not even in her twenties. Still, if they thought she was a hottie, maybe she should have used her face from one of those old photos for her avatar. Mind you, it would have been disturbing being herself behind the glasses but knowing that others only saw her youthful self. Creepy, as Lisa would have said. In any case, nobody would have recognized her in her twenties. Anybody who would was most likely dead.

After a while, hearing them still talking, her curiosity got the better of her. Out of sight in the kitchen, she listened intently. After all, who talked about her these days? Certainly nobody said anything flattering.

"Why do you act surprised?" Lisa continued. "Gran didn't always look like she looks today, you know. That stomach and those wrinkles...my mom says they happen to women as they get older. Men too. You think you're going to stay the same, but you don't. Change just creeps up on you, she says, and then one day you see a reflection of yourself in a mirror and you wonder, 'Who the hell is that?'"

"Is that what your mom says? How depressing."

Bertie had never believed she would get old until one day she discovered she was already there. It was a good thing she would soon be shedding her skin, becoming Vivienne, and leaving behind all that gross stomach and mass of wrinkles.

After Emory left, she asked Lisa how close her dad was to being ready with her realm. At his request, she had provided him with extra information about how she wanted her realm peopled and what buildings should furnish it. Besides the skaters, volleyball players, and muscle men, could he please add Merv, the lifeguard, whose picture she had taken in the seventies sitting atop his elevated chair scanning the sea for people in trouble, though more often focusing his binoculars on the female talent parading the beach? And what about Ramona, bent over a collapsible table with her tarot cards spread out before her, who could brighten or darken your day with a flip of a card? Bertie also suggested some of Vivienne's likes and dislikes, her biases and prejudices, her talents, and shortcomings. A couple of scars would now mark her blonde skin, she decided, but no tattoo. Who had tattoos in those days? Only sailors and thugs.

She became more and more impatient about getting her hands on the big guns of the metaverse and couldn't understand why Alex took such a long time.

"Do you think he will have the VR headset ready by my birthday?"

"I am not sure. Dad's been acting kinda weird recently. So distracted. He almost forgot his teacher/parent appointment with Mr. Hodges last week. Do you think he's got a girlfriend?" She watched Bertie's face to see her reaction.

"Of course not," Bertie assured her.

"Maybe they're getting divorced. Not that it's such a big issue," she bravely offered. "Half the kids in my class have divorced parents, even Emory."

"I doubt you need worry about divorce, sweetheart. I think your mom and dad are happy together."

"Yeah, maybe." She shrugged, pulled up her socks and returned the photo albums to their place on the bookshelves. "It's just that Mom keeps looking at herself in the mirror. She never used to do that."

"No, she never did. Not even as a teenager."

Lisa's comments worried her, and she wondered, had she missed something?

# CHAPTER 9

———

BERTIE'S BIRTHDAY ARRIVED AND WITH IT, ALEX'S HEAD-
set. Before giving it to her, he placed it on his head and drew
the digital boundaries that would prevent her from walking
into the study's furniture, namely Lennie's desk and chair, plus
bookshelves and a filing cabinet on wheels.

"It will feel just like a wall, if you bump into it," he warned
her, then lowered the virtual reality headset over Bertie's head,
enveloping her in darkness while he fiddled with the straps to
adjust it for a better fit. A bunch of her gray hair had become
entangled in the band, and he yanked it out without thinking.

"Since we put the battery at the back and redistributed the
weight, you will find it well-balanced," Alex said, proud of his
work.

She nodded, the slight movement almost toppling her as
she stood arms akimbo in the middle of Lennie's old study. Her
head felt heavy, certainly not balanced, and she was sure her
neck would ache by the end of the session. Lisa, who watched the
proceedings from the doorway, advised her to set her bare feet for
stability and to hold out her hands in front of her. It was a posi-

tion she had no problem maintaining, as it was not unlike how she made her way to the toilet at night when she needed to pee.

"Will these make Viv move backward and forward?" Bertie asked, pushing the levers on the controllers he now placed in her hands.

"Oh, so she's Viv now."

Bertie had taken to calling her proxy by the more intimate term because she and Alex had talked about her so much in the last months she had become a familiar. Who besides the two of them was even aware, for example, that syringes terrified her? Why she had listed that as one of Viv's phobias, Bertie didn't know. During her nursing life, she must have handled thousands of syringes.

"OK," she told Alex once she understood how to use the joystick to make Viv walk and the "O" inside the controllers to turn sharp right or left, "but how do I get her to talk if someone wants to have a conversation with her?"

Alex pointed out the built-in microphone and informed her she would use her own voice as Viv's.

"No way!" Bertie countered, the incongruity too much. "My old women's voice in the mouth of a 22-year-old?"

But the ever-resourceful Alex, ahead of the game as always, had attached a voice-disguising mechanism to the microphone so whenever Bertie spoke for Viv, her voice would be perky and sweet.

"Less serious," he said, making "serious" sound like a criticism.

"And when people wanted to speak to Viv, whether they were behind or alongside," he said, "she would hear them perfectly because the built-in headphones had immersive 3D audio. In fact, she could hear the slightest breeze rustling through grass, not that there was much of that on Venice Beach."

They covered the basics, but Alex still hadn't switched on the visuals in her headset. Only a black screen met her eyes.

"Enough already with the instructions," she finally said.

She was surprised at her own impatience, but she couldn't wait to experience her birthday present. She could always learn more about the operation as she went along and could see the connection between her actions and what happened in her virtual world. Following his directions, she aimed her trigger like a laser at the screen that now materialized before her, and when the words "Venice Beach" appeared on the menu, she clicked.

Lennie's study, like the living room, had huge windows looking out on the Puget Sound. As the program opened and the screen inside her headset came to life, she suddenly found herself facing not the Sound but the blue Pacific that, even without her glasses, looked more authentic than in real life. While perfectly curved rollers following some heavenly pattern crashed on the shore, seagulls in search of fishy treasures called to one another in high-pitched shrieks before dumpster-diving the garbage bins that dotted the beach.

In LA it was 3:30 on an April afternoon and a vibrating orange ball shone overhead. There was no "cruelest month" in LA. Summer ruled every day, the entire place sun bleached, the orb's munificence warming everything and everyone, including Ocean Front Walk that ran along the beach for over two miles, and where a river of people now moved in both directions. Unlike in the games that Bertie played where armies of metallic enemies approached her with blood-curdling screams, their weapons drawn, their fangs unsheathed, here she faced only skaters, bicyclers, runners, and pedestrians, all of them in shorts or jeans, wanting to see and be seen. She could not believe how realistic everything looked, how familiar. There sat Ramona (or someone like her) solemnly reading her tarot cards, and to her left, the Birkenstock-sandaled seller of tie-dyed T-shirts bending over her wares and showing off her slender thighs. Colorful bungalows lined the beach and among them...yes, the very same cute pink house where her friend Christine and she had stayed in 1974, not quite in the exact position she remembered, but then, was she going to measure yards? Probably the cottage no longer existed, but thanks to superimposing in the metaverse whatever you liked on the real, Alex had resurrected it.

From a boom box on the shoulder of a Latino avatar, she could hear Paul and John bellowing about "Lady Madonna" needing to pay the rent. She hadn't seen a boom box in years and wondered how many of those young men who thought themselves cool dudes with their blaring music now concealed hearing aids beneath their few gray strands.

A dozen or so other people lay on the beach or paraded around showing off their bods to one another. Like those walking, running, or skating, they were not live, just part of the scenery, empty shells until players adopted them. Alex called them his NPCs, non-player characters, whom he might bring into the action at some point, or not. Viv too was not yet live. At the moment, he informed Bertie through the microphone, the Latino was the only live avatar in her realm.

"See the light above his head? It's just like in the games you play with Lisa."

"So, who is he?" she asked. "I mean, who is the Latino in real life?"

"Nobody. Just someone from my office, one of our team members. I can't risk anyone from outside seeing how far we've come. Look, I could have used old APIs to create your metaverse, but they could be vulnerable to bad actors who could hijack my product. There are a few new developments that are just so exciting!"

"APIs? You mean points of entry through which someone can access and control bits and pieces of the larger program?"

He stared at her, impressed. Bertie explained she had done a bit of reading. Besides, she slowly picked up the lingo from him and Lisa, even if she didn't fully grasp the meaning of the words, given her lack of context. Her newly acquired vocabulary, however, did not alleviate Alex's worries about espionage.

"I'm taking a bit of a risk here, you realize, so please be as discreet as you can, Bertie. You know the tech companies are all in competition with one another and spies are out there just dying to lift someone else's ideas about the metaverse."

As he said the words, she visualized Daru and Marion blithely talking on top of their voices about her metaverse. Not that they knew anyone active in cutting-edge technology, but Daru still had many of her old colleagues in the media. Who knew how a throwaway sentence might get picked up by a curious professional? She would have to remind them again that her entire life was at stake.

When Alex ran his fingers through his hair, she noticed how thin it had become. He was no longer a kid, and with the magic number fifty just on the horizon, she imagined he felt pressure to make his mark. The recent developments he felt proud of involved camera work. With most VR headsets, you had to erect tracking cameras around the room to capture the movement of your body in real time to transfer it to your avatar. It was an amazing feat in itself, but Alex and his team had come up with a way of using sensors *inside* the headset, thus eliminating the need for external ones. So, if she got it into her head to take off her underwear, for example, Viv would repeat her movements and remove hers. If she stuck out her tongue, Viv would do the same. How this was accomplished, she could not begin to fathom.

"So then, if I do something embarrassing in my metaverse, your office buddy will see me?"

"Afraid so."

When she told Marion later, she said, "Not just his office buddy; Alex will probably peep at you too."

Bertie told her not to be disgusting. Trust her to think of something so weird.

"But the good news is," Alex continued, "he won't know who you are. He'll only see Vivienne."

"Lucky me! OK, so where is she already? Where is Vivienne?"

"Do you want to see what she looks like before I connect you? Perhaps get to know what it feels like to be her?"

For a moment, Bertie felt nervous, as if she were about to meet…what? herself? her ghost? the personification of her earlier life? Like a science-fiction ghoul, she would step into Viv's body, "embodying" her, as Alex described it. If what he said proved accurate, Bertie would not merely be pretending to be Viv, she would become her. She would be Viv.

Her avatar, who remained "lifeless" until they connected, stood in front of Maxine's, the swimsuit store, looking at rows of triangular bikini bottoms displayed like folded, overlapping handkerchiefs. In her flared blue jeans and low-cut peasant blouse sporting puffed sleeves embroidered with red flowers to match the ones on her jeans, Viv looked even better than Bertie had imagined her. On her feet, she wore the ubiquitous Indian leather sandals they all loved in the seventies, and which, coincidentally, were also the only ones she could afford on her nurse's salary. Ten bangles jangled on Viv's right arm and from her ear lobes hung the silver peace symbols that represented Bertie's ideology. She could have been any of a dozen young women Bertie remembered from her vacation at Venice Beach all those years ago.

She stared at Viv's reflection in the window—her perfect nose with its delicate nostrils, the equally spaced eyes that seemed too big for her face; they had all been made to Bertie's specifications. She felt like she had produced a made-to-order child. The knowledge unsettled her, sending a little *frisson* down her neck. How long before they made customized babies in the real world by tweaking DNA? High intelligence—check! Smooth olive skin—check! Legs, firm and straight—all just menu options, like the choices at TechTown Café, completed with a tip.

Though Vivienne looked nothing like her, Bertie thought of her as her doppelgänger and felt a peculiar umbilical connection. She seemed so innocent, so defenseless out there, unable to act or protect herself without her controller. Her life lay in Bertie's hands. She would have no redress. Once they connected, whatever Bertie did, she had to do. She could not fight Bertie, spear her, or knife her, as avatars could do in the games she played with Lisa. In this new game, their relationship was inequitable. Bertie held all the power.

"Why don't you touch her?" Alex's voice intruded into her Venice Beach world. "Get comfortable and see what she feels like. Touch her arms."

What did he mean, "touch her arms." Wouldn't she be touching her own? Or rather, the air? She lifted her right arm and gingerly dropped her fingers onto Viv's skin just below the edge of her sleeve. Her rational brain imagined how ridiculous she must look to Alex as she grabbed at the empty air in the space below her. She knew there was nothing there, but Alex urged her on, telling her to keep going, keep touching, so she could familiarize herself with Viv's body before she appropriated it as her own. So, she continued patting and stroking, running her fingers around Viv's elbow, feeling where her funny bone stood out even with her arm dangling. Although well-endowed in bust and butt, as Daru and Marion had suggested, Viv's arms were slender. When Bertie slipped her fingers between hers, they felt long and delicate, her nails short and square, just like her own had been as a nurse. With Alex still coaching her, encouraging her to get to know her avatar, she lifted Viv's other hand and familiarized herself in the same way, tapping and stroking her fingers, her own catching on a roughened ridge near her wrist bone, one of the two scars she had chosen for her avatar. She wondered what painful mishap had caused this one and felt sympathy for Viv, even wanting to protect her.

"Hey," she greeted her.

Through Viv's eyes, which were now her own eyes, she looked at her reflection in the store window, and bit by bit started to see not Viv and Bertie, not them, but a single "her." A "she" with thin arms and delicate fingers, a scar on her wrist. Alex had said the embodiment would take place gradually, but Bertie already felt as if her old self receded, losing ground to what she saw in front of her, no matter how impossible it all seemed.

"OK," she told Alex. "Let's do it," though she surely knew she had a way to go before she embodied Viv entirely.

When a click sounded, she shifted her head slightly and Viv shifted hers simultaneously. When she cleared her throat, the sound emerged from Viv's mouth, and she could see in the glass reflection how her lips opened. It should have felt strange, bizarre even, this state of being herself, but not her. For a moment, she thought of the movie *Being John Malkovich* and wondered if Viv had found a portal into her mind. Or was it rather that she had found one into hers? She shifted her weight and watched Viv transfer hers from one leg to the other. Her knee bent slightly and just for a second, Bertie mistakenly thought she had done it herself. The more they moved together, the closer they became. Slowly but surely, if Alex was correct, she would assume a second skin, a new digital skin.

"So, I am going to leave you to it then," Alex said, pulling on his hoodie and heading for the door. "Call me if you have any problems."

And with that, Lisa and he went home for supper, and she was left alone with Viv, taking her first tentative steps into a foreign world that didn't even exist.

That night, Marion and Daru took her out for dinner to celebrate her seventy-fifth. Most of the restaurants in South Lake Union were deserted because the techies who worked in the neighborhood escaped it in their off-hours and fled to Pike Street to play at being bohemian. Perhaps the change of scenery helped steel them for the all-nighters they needed to pull most other times. On the other hand, maybe they weren't there just to pretend. Maybe they broke out of their cocoons as raving butterflies, kicking aside all those zeros and ones, ready to party.

Only four other tables were occupied at Gerrard's. After three miserable years of Covid, many neighborhood restaurants still struggled to find their economic feet. Some reduced their hours or opened only at lunchtime when they could be sure of attracting techie customers. Gerrard's, their favorite, had survived, but with so many tables empty, the place wore a despondent air, the feel of a much-hyped party to which nobody had come. Though the waiters tried their hardest to be upbeat, their smiles seemed ersatz, given a limited number of wait staff had already been trimmed and they probably waited in trepidation for their own dismissal. Tonight, however, the emptiness of the restaurant meant the three women could bag a good table, away from the door and other diners. Bertie could hardly wait to tell Marion and Daru about her metaverse experience earlier in the day, her head being full of Vivienne and what she was going to have her do. Wasn't it her birthday too? In a sense, that night was the beginning of her life in the metaverse of LA.

They had hardly taken off their masks and ordered some wine, when Daru started crying.

"I'm so sorry, Bertie," she sniffed, tears streaming down her face. "I just can't help it. I wanted to be happy on your special day, but no matter what I do, the tears keep coming. I can't control them." She dabbed under her mascaraed eyes with the white napkin, then looked in horror at the black traces they left behind. "I wonder if the restaurant can wash these out?"

They had expected Daru to bounce back once her mourning period was over. After all, she'd had two years of Aditya's last-stage cancer to get used to the idea of his passing, and the previous week, had completed the final ritual required of her, namely, giving alms to the needy. On the assigned day for the performance, she, Marion, and Bertie had dressed in white, then walked down Third Avenue handing out one hundred food packages they had prepared earlier. Each bag also contained a five-dollar bill.

"Just enough for a bottle of Thunderbird or a lick of fentanyl," Marion commented.

With her palms pressing against her eyes as if she could rub the tears away, Daru sobbed about how guilty she felt. "I should have been kinder to Aditya and more loving when he was in so much pain."

"You couldn't have been more kind," Marion interjected. "And patient. God, you were patient, always responding to his calls and speaking soothingly to him when he became agitated."

Bertie put her arm around Daru's thin shoulders, reminding her of how she had run their home and finances alone, and how she had dealt with Aditya's doctors, and made sure he took his medications every four hours.

"Remember how you sat up with him night after night when he thrashed in pain and couldn't sleep?"

"Yes, but at the same time I was thinking 'Die already!'" She broke out in a new bout of sobbing, subjecting the napkin to yet another despoiling.

"Of course, you wanted him dead, Daru. If getting better wasn't an option," Marion said, "who wouldn't want the pain to stop? After my husband took off with his floozy, I spent two whole years thinking 'Die already, you shit!'"

"But I loved my husband," Daru protested, twisting the napkin until the stains were no longer visible.

"I loved mine too. Once."

"Guys," Bertie said, "it's natural sometimes to hate the person you love."

"Is that right, Dear Carolyn Hax?" Marion mocked her for sounding like the *Times* advice columnist. Even Daru attempted a laugh.

"Look, I'm not trying to be holier-than-thou. There were moments when I hated Lennie too. Plenty of them." She thought of those parties they attended where he would wallow in the attention of other women, as if they were his due. He was insufferable. And that one time he...no, she wouldn't go there now. She didn't want to be reminded. "All I'm trying to say is most women struggle with anger and hatred. Don't think our partners don't feel the same, for many reasons, some of which we probably never sense."

"Mine once told me he watched me when I slept and hated me. I have no idea what I'd done to him"—Marion simulated an innocent face—"but all I could think about was how I must have looked with my mouth hanging open, drool rolling down one side, a cheek squashed against the pillow. You know how when you press fat at one end, it bulges out the other."

"How cruel," Daru commiserated.

"The important thing," Bertie said, not wanting to spiral further into such morbid thoughts, "is we have one another. Look at us. We are survivors. Husbands die, husbands run away, and we are still here. Not quite what we were and lugging around a few extra pounds and pains, but we're here."

"Like *The Golden Girls*, we will be here to care for each other until the end," Marion added. "If one of us gets sick, the other two will care for her. That's the way it will work."

"Darn right!" she confirmed, feeling her own eyes well up.

"I'll drink to that." Daru lifted her glass, *her* tears gone. "To friendship! May we go into that dark night gently!"

"And together!" Marion and Bertie chipped in simultaneously.

# CHAPTER 10

———

AS SHE GOT TO KNOW VIV AND REFAMILIARIZED HERSELF with Venice Beach, a new sense of excitement and discovery suffused Bertie. The more times she entered the metaverse, the greater became her enjoyment at being there. She felt as if she were embarking on a new story, whose trajectory she did not know, but which she would follow to its end. No matter where it took her, she would throw herself into the journey, immersing herself in this three-dimensional world, even if she possessed only the vaguest idea of the technology that drove it in the real world. At least, she knew more than she did six months ago when the term "metaverse" could have been an exotic word from a foreign language. How grateful she felt to her son-in-law for giving her this opportunity to dip a toe into the stream.

She adjusted her headset now and brought Venice Beach to life. Her screen lit up with bright sunshine, revealing a postcard scene of beachgoers drifting across the glass as if in one of those snow domes that had recently been shaken. Among them she spied Viv. That will never do, she thought. Viv walked as if she barely moved a muscle. Like characters in some games

Bertie played with Lisa, Viv's feet flew just above the level of the street, as if she were some angel and not a young woman with big boobs and a puppet-master who wanted her to have fun. Wasn't that the point, after all? No way would something exciting happen if she simply blended into the background. Bertie switched on the controls, taking ownership of Viv. Immediately, Viv's body responded. It was as if she had infused her with red blood. Her shoulders straightened, her head lifted, and she looked around, taking in her surroundings like a newly arrived tourist marveling at the ocean that lay spread out in its aquamarine best. With her unblemished face and blonde hair swinging around her shoulders, she must have looked fantastic.

She still walked like an automaton, however, so, remembering what Alex had taught her about skeletal tracking, and assuming the sensors would follow whatever part of her body she moved if she adjusted their angle, Bertie straightened her legs and sashayed her hips just slightly, not overdoing it lest Viv look like she tried too hard. The seventies were laid back and nobody wanted to appear contrived. With the VR headset on, and looking through Viv's eyes, she walked down to the water. She couldn't see Viv's body, but she could sense the way she moved. The two of them were still separate, and Bertie imagined Viv's butt shifting from side to side in her tight jeans, each cheek provoking the other in a battle for space. Her straightened legs, however, were not quite right for walking on sand, so Bertie bent a little at the knees and Viv moved much more realistically, her heels digging into the sand.

How those sensors could transfer her ridiculous septuagenarian sashay to the sexy young hips of her avatar however lay beyond Bertie's understanding. Did they pick up the spinal and bone movement through the loose flesh and bulging waistline? Emboldened by this success, she had Viv pivot and wave at the lifeguard perched on his elevated chair, scanning the surf. Though "Merv" never responded—he was a nonactivated player—she felt she made progress.

When Viv reached the water's edge, she turned her to the left before the foam from the breaking waves could wash over her feet. She needed more walking practice before she could take off Viv's sandals and have her wade, but fortunately the excellent design of Alex's system kept her walking in whatever way she last set her. Bertie didn't need to make continuous body movements. Only when something changed in her environment, like a new person or a beach chair blocked her way, did Bertie step in to reorient her.

In what Alex called "real time rendering," today was slightly windier than yesterday, and the waves rolled in bigger and crashed more noisily, just as they had on this day in April 1974. She took Alex's word for it, but she wondered whether she should access some of this information in advance so she could make plans, in case it rained, for example. But then, winter was over and when did it ever rain in an LA spring?

If only Marion and Daru could see what she saw. They had helped her create Viv, but she couldn't invite them to join her yet. For the moment, it was only she, Alex, and his office buddy, whose avatar just happened to walk toward Viv now. He still bore his boom box aloft, but this time, "Somebody To Love" by Jefferson Airplane rang from his loudspeakers, growing in decibels as he got closer. Without realizing it, Bertie hummed the tune, and then she heard the same sound coming out of Viv's mouth. She moved her shoulders in time to the music and assumed Viv did too, though she couldn't see her. The Latino drew level.

"Looking cool, babe!" he announced, winking at her. Bertie covered her mouth to stop herself from guffawing. People talked like that in the sixties and seventies, but it sounded so anachronistic now, it made her giggle. Had Alex coached him in boomer lingo?

Lennie, the wordsmith, had never used "groovy" or "mellow" or "dig it," or any other words created by the zeitgeist of the time. He never threw out snatches of half sentences either. His thoughts emerged fully formed in whole paragraphs, sounding sometimes like songs or novels, depending on his mood. Listening to him, she sometimes felt bathed in language, drenched, massaged, attacked, soothed, and she would quickly clamp her lips to his to interrupt.

Viv, however, had no problem with the Latino's "looking cool, babe." She and the boom box player communicated on the same linguistic wavelength, and any feminist objections Bertie might have had about the male gaze never made it through the affection she felt as they checked each other out.

"Thanks, dude." Viv smiled back. "Not bad yourself," Bertie said through Viv's lips.

OMG! Where did that come from? She felt blood rush to her cheeks, reminding her of stupid ripostes she had made in her twenties. Tech buddy must have felt as embarrassed as she because he walked off, raising his hand in a kind of half wave. Who was he imagining behind Viv's avatar? Or did he see only Viv?

Closer to the cafés and beach houses, two body builders squatted under the weight of dumbbells. Neither were live avatars, but they could move monotonously up and down, distinguishing them from other NPCs relegated to floating ghost-like through the ether. She walked Viv in their direction, and they stood there for a while not doing anything until she decided, fuck, this is really boring. Where had the Latino gone and why wasn't he chatting her up? Maybe she needed to plan Viv's day, create opportunities for her, just like she would have for herself, rather than wait for things to happen. We are still new at this partnership, she told Viv, but once we get the hang of things, I promise you our lives will get more exciting. With images of dancing and cavorting in her head, she switched off her headset and put her avatar to sleep until the next day.

●●

When she emerged from Lennie's study, Lisa was already there doing her homework on her laptop.

"What are you working on?" she asked. "Can I help?"

She enjoyed going over Lisa's history lessons with her, retelling events as stories and filling them in with details of ordinary life at the time. Given her seventy-five years, a bit of that ordinary life had been experienced by her personally. Lisa mumbled something noncommittal but didn't even bother lifting her head. Perhaps it wasn't unusual behavior for a 13-year-old, but Lisa always talked to her.

"Is something wrong?" Bertie asked.

"You'll find out soon enough." Lisa shrugged her shoulders.

That was sufficient to scare the bejeezus out of her. What could be wrong? Had Arielle been involved in an accident? Had Alex lost his job? Had Lisa failed an exam? She knew she wouldn't get anything more out of her granddaughter in this mood, so she went to the kitchen and started brewing some tea. While she waited and imagined the worst, she sprayed Lennie's photograph frame with Windex and erased Lisa's smudged fingerprints from the glass. She walked around the apartment aimlessly, fidgeting here and there, straightening the pictures on the wall, folding the clean laundry, when Alex arrived early to pick up Lisa. On opening the door, however, she saw it wasn't just Alex standing there but Arielle too.

"Mom, we have something to tell you." Her daughter walked in and edged her toward the sofa. "Sit down."

Alex, meanwhile, stood by the window staring at the Olympic Mountains in the distance. It was a clear day and still light out. April was Seattle's best month, though this year temperatures had remained low, dissuading the mountain peaks from jettisoning their snowy caps.

"But did you know"—she suddenly started talking about the weather, hoping perhaps to stave off whatever bad news he and Arielle were about to anoint her with—"that despite the cold, there's blossoming and birthing all over the city. Yes, really. Most gardens sprout at the very least a spattering of daffodils and tulips. And in the Arboretum...you've probably seen this yourselves...showers of cherry blossoms on the walkways. Just the other day when I was out strolling there, I saw Japanese women posing beneath the cherry trees and their friends snapping pictures of them for Instagram."

Lisa sat with her back to them, pretending not to listen.

"Mom," Arielle said quietly, scattering Bertie's cherry blossoms, "about birthing..."

"Yes, just the other day, the cat in my neighbor's yard..."

"Mom, I'm pregnant."

It took Bertie a moment to take in her stark, unflowery words with her generation's fear of unexpected pregnancies. It had been thirteen years since Lisa's birth, and though Arielle and Alex had tried to give Lisa a sibling, there had been multiple miscarriages. Arielle had finally thrown in the towel and accepted she would never have another child. A pregnancy, therefore, was the last thing Bertie had expected. Despite her relief it wasn't something else, she hesitated before reacting, not knowing if a bun in the oven represented good news or bad. Did she jump up in excitement, which is what she felt?

Or did she commiserate? There was, after all, Arielle's career to consider. How would she manage her pediatric practice with a baby in tow? Would Alex change diapers? Would he do the night feedings?

"We'd given up using contraception, thinking that nothing could happen after all this time," Arielle explained. "I mean, I am already forty-five, which I thought much too old to get pregnant, but then..." Her lips trembled at the corners, and Bertie held her breath. Then, Arielle broke into a huge smile.

"Oh, sweetheart, I am so happy for you. What incredible news!"

She threw her arms about her daughter, then went to hug Alex, congratulating him. Though he tried to hide it, his face wore that look of pride in fulfilling his manhood that one often saw in men, no matter how many children they had already sired.

"So, how far along are you?"

"Six months."

"Six, already?"

"Well, we didn't want to tell you before we knew for certain the baby was here to stay. Not that it is ever a sure thing, of course." She knocked on the wooden arm of Lennie's old chair. "Something can still go wrong."

"Nothing will go wrong."

She took Arielle's face in her hands, seeing in it the little girl who always expected the worst to happen. When Bertie and Lennie just hoped for the best, it was Arielle who organized and planned. Her pessimism had made her the best-prepared Girl Scout in her division. A picture of her daughter's 6-year-old self waiting in the kitchen already neatly dressed in her uniform, backpack ready, her pens organized by color, flitted through Bertie's mind.

"I still can't believe it. You've made me a grandma again."

"Yup." Alex nodded. "To keep you on your toes, Bertie. Can't have you slacking now that Lisa is thirteen."

So, she would be babysitting. Not that she had any objection. In fact, the idea thrilled her though she doubted she would get on her arthritic hands and knees to play "Horsie" this time around. During Lisa's infancy, Arielle had worked part-time, and between her and Alex, they managed to juggle things. Whenever they needed a break, Bertie and Lennie would drive down from Vancouver and hold the fort, but when Lennie retired from his position with the governor, Arielle petitioned them: Would they consider moving to Seattle and helping with Lisa so she could return to full-time work? That was in 2015, when they were all in love with Obama and suddenly America seemed like the place to be. Yes, they knew about the terrible shootings, the racism, and anti-Semitism, the groups that screamed, "You will not replace us!" But better angels had won out in America and Obama demonstrated what was possible if people only wanted it enough. That, together with their joy to be part of their granddaughter's life, to be able to laugh with her, and cherish her, was enough for them to pack up their things, sadly take leave of their friends, and apply for Lennie's visa. With Vancouver only a three-hour drive away, they could always visit the old home.

They never looked back.

Now, staring at her granddaughter about to be a big sister, she felt grateful they had made the decision. She kissed the top of Lisa's head and said congratulations, but her granddaughter ignored her.

"She's upset," her father said.

"I am not upset. I'm embarrassed."

"C'mon, Lisa, you know that parents have sex."

"Of course, I know that, but not when they are so old! Almost fifty! Now, all my friends will know you are still doing it."

Bertie wanted to take her in her arms and tell her it was OK, that everything would be alright.

"Think of your friends' moms who had second marriages in their forties," she said, "and then had a baby with their new husbands. Even old people have sex. If I had a partner, I would also have sex."

Lisa swung around on her seat with such an amazed look that Arielle burst out laughing and Bertie felt terrible for her granddaughter. She hated that something she had said made her the butt of laughter.

"Would you really?" She looked incredulous. "And with someone other than Gramps?"

What to say? Lennie was no longer here, so yes, it would be with someone else, not that it was an option in the immediate future. Men were not knocking on her door looking for a friend with benefits.

"Lisa," she began, "even old ladies..."

Sometimes when she spoke to her granddaughter, it was like having a conversation with a grown-up friend. Then there were occasions when she responded like a child. Now was such an occasion, and she had misjudged it.

"How could you?" Her young face puckered, her dark eyebrows meeting in the middle, like Frida's. The disappointment showed; it needed no more words.

"Lisa..." she tried again, but the keeper of Lennie's flame had already risen and was walking toward the door.

●●

The following Monday afternoon, having left Lisa and her parents to talk things out over the weekend, Bertie suggested she and Lisa pop down to TechTown and have her bagel there.

"And a blueberry smoothie?" Lennie had taught her well.

"Sure," she said, giving her a hug.

A few minutes later, sitting in her and Marion's usual corner, she watched Lisa's lovely little face pulling on the straw, her eyes focusing on the blueberry-and-banana drink from beneath long black eyelashes. Tom didn't have the raisin-cinnamon bagel she loved, so she reluctantly accepted a sesame one, the seeds from which now lay scattered across the table. With her baby finger, she moved them into little piles as if she were amassing armed forces.

"Your mom says the baby will be a girl," Bertie said, trying to recalibrate their relationship after her mistake last night.

What had she been thinking to put such an image in her granddaughter's head? Now, she wanted her to see the new family group as the beginning of an exciting chapter in her life, a time of self-discovery and that intriguing love/hate emotion that siblings sometimes talk about. Of that, Bertie knew nothing, for her mom had died young, before she could give her a sister or brother to either love or hate, but how she dreamed of having one. Another person to play with? Such fun it would have been. But it was not in the cards, and her dad never remarried until after she left home, having taken it into his head that only he knew how to care for her.

"I was so lonely growing up without a sister," she shared with Lisa.

"Well, I'm never lonely!" She crossed her arms and scowled. Then, perhaps feeling a tad contrite about not being more sympathetic, she added, "Anyhow, you have Marion and Daru now. They are your sisters."

How right she was. The sisters of her old age, for whom she was daily grateful; without whom her life might have followed a downward spiral after Lennie's death. Not that she was ever dependent on Lennie for her friendships, but some things change after so many years of marriage, and you cannot always understand them yourself.

"But getting back to *your* life," Bertie reminded her, "you do know, don't you, that you will be your sister's role model? She will mimic everything you do. She will want to be just like you."

"Why would she want to be like me?" Lisa pulled a face.

"Because you are fun to be with and everyone likes you."

"No, they don't! They think I'm a dork."

"Emory doesn't."

"That's because he's also a dork."

"Well, you are a beautiful, talented dork who plays a wicked clarinet."

She winked at her granddaughter over the rim of her coffee, eliciting a reluctant smile before Lisa resumed her "I will not be amused" face. Still, encouraged by her hint of a smile, Bertie talked, edging around her upset at her parents' "doing it" at almost fifty, an upset which she now thought didn't ring quite true, given how worldly and sophisticated Lisa could be when she wanted. But perhaps knowledge remained an abstraction until it touched one's own family and became personal. Not that that thought, an abstraction itself, passed her lips to Lisa. Instead, she spoke to her of the sadness each of her mother's miscarriages had wrought, a sadness Arielle had hidden from her daughter so as not to burden her. And did she remember the other clarinetist in the school orchestra? What was her name? Was it Klara or Claire? She had a baby sibling at least ten years younger than herself.

As she talked, she noticed how Lisa retreated into herself— her chin nestling into her neck, her bottom lip nipping at her top, her eyes cast down, unseeing. Anything Bertie said seemed to waft by her, unheard.

"Wasn't I enough for them?" she suddenly blurted out. "That's why they had to have another child?"

Her questions came accompanied by just the slightest hint of tears, which she quickly blinked away, but not before Bertie had felt the pain of her words as she realized that such thoughts must have been circling her granddaughter's mind for days, eating her up.

"I mean," she continued, trying to avoid looking at Bertie directly, "if they really loved me, they wouldn't need to have another child after all these years. Would they?"

Her heart ached for her young granddaughter.

"What are you saying, Lisa? Your parents adore you. They love you. You know that, sweetheart."

"But maybe thirteen years of living with me did not give them what they expected from parenthood? I mean I'm not beautiful, brilliant, or popular."

"Listen, sweetheart, you are all those things, and your parents couldn't be more grateful for the person you have become. That's part of the reason why they wanted another child. Your thirteen years have given them so much pride and joy—*naches*, as my *bubbe* would have said—that at their ages they're prepared to have another child just so they can experience you all over again. Of course, nobody can ever replace you, but they want another child just like you." She took a breath. "Lisa, if you had been a disappointment or made their lives hell, they would have had second thoughts about this pregnancy. They might even have considered abortion."

At the word "abortion," Lisa's head popped up, at attention. "What did you say?"

Had she put a possibility into her head, where no such possibility existed? Arielle was in her third trimester, due in three months. As she searched Lisa's eyes, however, she realized her mistake. Her granddaughter's response to the word had not been to see abortion as a way out of her doubt, but rather a reaction of protective shock. What? You wouldn't dare touch my baby sister. Bertie took it as a hopeful sign, of a slight move away from the dark thoughts crushing her own spirit to the beginning of an acceptance. So, though Lisa's eyes remained downcast, and she blew bubbles in her blueberry smoothie, Bertie kept talking. With time, it became easier to imagine another small person existing within the circle of the family, a little girl whose eyes would light up at the sight of her big sister.

"Maybe you will play 'Moonglow' for the baby," she suggested, checking the waters for shoals.

"On my clarinet?"

When she offered a half smile and envisioned just such a scene, Bertie felt encouraged to continue. "Or perhaps you can teach yourself some lullabies. Like 'Hush Little Baby, Don't You Cry,' you know the one that goes, 'Papa's going to give you a mockingbird.' I used to sing that to you when you were small. You wouldn't go to bed unless I did."

She started to sing softly, "Hush little baby," but for some reason instead of the descending notes of the sweet "don't you cry," her voice lifted á la Joan Baez and she segued into "All My Trials."

"What was that? I like it."

"No, no, the words are too sad, not what you want to sing to a baby at all."

"Well, can you just hum the rest of it? I like minor key songs."

Bertie didn't get beyond three bars before she wanted to cry.

"Look, I'll play it for you when we get home. 'Summertime' too. It's also derived from the gospel hymn 'All My Trials.'"

"I already know how to play 'Summertime,'" and she put an imaginary clarinet to her lips.

Her fingers with their purple polka-dotted nails struck invisible pads.

"Way to go," barista Tom shouted over his steaming Gaggia machine.

Lisa grinned, not at all embarrassed to be playing air-clarinet. Soon, she'd forgotten about the impending arrival of her sister and chatted away about her jazz band and who she thought were the better players and who needed to be evicted before they dragged the whole crew down. By the time they returned to the apartment, only music filled her head. She had hardly touched a kiss to Lennie's picture before she picked up her clarinet and started practicing.

# CHAPTER 11

———

BERTIE'S RESEARCH WAS GOING WELL, AND EVERY DAY SHE became more proficient at controlling her realm. Though some glitches persisted before she got Viv's movements right, her avatar could now kick off her sandals and seductively push a wisp of hair behind her ear, that last feat taking some doing because Bertie had to allow the sensors to trace her fingers from all angles before Viv could replicate the movement.

Looking at her own age-spotted hands, studying the phalanges and metacarpals of her arthritic digits that despite their swelling and crookedness nevertheless functioned as intended, she marveled at this human tool. Even if she could no longer slide a button through a buttonhole or twist the childproof cap on her Ambien, the tips of her fingers with their density of nerve endings remained the most sensitive part of her body, her sense of touch as young as ever.

Now, if she could only train Viv to lift both hands and pull her hair through an elastic band to make a ponytail. The problem was that she couldn't see if Viv did it correctly; she could only surmise by the feel of her movements and perhaps the boom box guy's reactions, though she doubted he would have said anything if the elastic held only four strands and left the rest of Viv's hair dangling.

At first, she thought that by switching off Viv's live connection her avatar would come into full focus, but as soon as she did that, Viv simply reverted to an untethered, unlive, floating being.

"Can't you do something about it?" she asked Alex, already looking the proverbial gift horse in the mouth. "I really would love to watch Viv in action at the same time as seeing through her eyes as if I were her."

He mumbled something about losing the direct interactive feel but, being Alex and always up to a challenge, he said he would think about it. A week later, he had invented a red switch that allowed Bertie, if only briefly, to toggle between Viv and herself, so besides viewing Viv's admirer, she could also appreciate what he faced when he stared bashfully at Viv. By checking in her side-view mirror, as she liked to call it, Bertie could see how well her movements translated to Viv's.

In fact, she felt confident about getting the hang of things. But then, from a preloaded balance on her phone app that allowed her to buy clothes for Viv online, she purchased a pair of fashionable, big, brown sunglasses and soon realized that some actions just defied imitation. Viv's sunglasses refused to stay put and snow-plowed down her nose before landing in the sand.

"Your fault for giving her such a small nose," Alex said when she recounted her experience to him later.

But that was what people admired in the seventies, just like big hairdos. It didn't help that she couldn't fit her sunglasses on her cyborg-like head to show Viv and had to make do with simply holding them where the end of her nose stuck out from the VR headset. She practiced taking the glasses off and putting them back on, and even clenching the end of one plastic arm between her teeth, but Viv had so many mishaps with that last action that, despite how sexy it might have looked, Bertie gave up on the idea and just hung the glasses from the front of Viv's blouse.

Meantime, she had also tired of Viv wearing the same embroidered top and flared jeans. She picked out a pretty summer dress which showed off Viv's golden tan, then searched for a swimsuit. Not that Viv would be going swimming or surfing anytime soon, but she might well want to wade in the shallows and feel the wet sand squelch between her toes. The red bikini Bertie finally decided on came with a red floral caftan cover-up. While those few purchases did not a wardrobe make, they would suffice to keep Viv going in seventies fashion for as long as Bertie kept at what she liked to think of as her "research." Knowing now that Alex could improve her little world if she pestered him enough, Bertie took a shot at getting him to persuade merchants to lower their prices on goods they sold in the meta-market but, sad to say, her son-in-law's influence did not stretch that far. There was no market bargaining in this simulated world.

Sometimes she wished Michael could see her setup. With his "Promises, Promises," the concierge had virtually denied the metaverse would ever materialize in his lifetime. "Too many competing companies," he had insisted. "Probably won't ever get off the ground." To be fair, her metaverse certainly could have done with more tweaking. Delays sometimes made the action seem jerky, like the movements of a robot (Alex called it the refresh rate, which sometimes did not register high enough), and now and then, when she zoomed too close, the 3D environment broke down into lower fidelity, confronting her with straight lines and triangles that interrupted her magical world. Just when she identified with Viv, and feeling like she was her in some instances, exposure to the inner workings of her realm would burst her otherworldly bubble.

Despite such problems, which Alex had assured her when she reported them to him that his people were already at work on effective solutions, the point as far as Michael was concerned was that *her* metaverse, at least, was indeed up and running.

Even if she had wanted to gloat to Michael, however, he no longer controlled Mariela Plaza's lobby. When a competing student in the same small field looked to pip him at the post, he had finally resigned to finish his dissertation. Competition will do that, catapult you into the race, willing or not. If you didn't wish to see all your work going down the drain, you had no option but to compete. Which is why she had great hopes the tech world would iron out all the metaverse's wrinkles. Each company wanted to reach the post first, but to do so it could not go alone. It must negotiate.

Thanks to Alex, she and Viv had at their disposal the simulated little pink bungalow where she and Christine had stayed so many years ago. Just two rooms and a kitchen, it nevertheless gave them a base from which to operate and a place where they could store their things. It also offered privacy when they needed to undress. Back in her day in the real cottage, Christine, who had remained faithful to her fiancé the entire two weeks of their vacation, never had need of that privacy. Only Bertie, at last legally freed from her ball and chain, sought it when some charmer caught her fancy.

In retrospect, she and Christine were an odd couple vacationing together; she, about to enter a marriage, Bertie, having just left one. Yet somehow, it had worked out, and they had both returned home refreshed and ready for the next stages of their lives. Christine's stages, however, did not extend past her fifty-second birthday when a drunken driver snuffed out what remained of her existence. Overnight, she was gone, leaving a gaping hole in Bertie's life. How Christine would have loved to see this re-creation of their Venice Beach time, when the measuring tape of their lifespans still lay rolled up ahead of them, its remaining length unknown.

Now, moving Viv around in this re-creation, she kept being reminded of Christine, the way she loved to stride the full length of the beach through the surf, enjoying the feel of the wet sand on her soles as her heels dug in, leaving temporary footprints, size seven. Sitting in cafés sipping her salt-rimmed margarita and watching the world go by also appealed to her. Without cell phones to monopolize her attention then, she maintained a running commentary about each person she saw, imagining a man's personality from the way he turned his head, shrugged, smiled, or used his hands. She had a sharp eye for recognizing a mensch. Her husband-to-be proved evidence of that.

Bertie seated Viv at the kind of outdoor café that Christine liked, though this one, Barbie's, hadn't been there in their day. Another one of Alex's simulations. Now, instead of wandering around aimlessly, Viv sat back, relaxed, and smiled occasionally at the Rastafarian playing his bongo drums opposite the café. With his eyes closed and his head back, he looked lost in his personal metaverse.

She rearranged the front of Viv's caftan to reveal more of her crossed leg when who should stop by this time without his boom box. His name was Jorge, but incongruously he spoke with a pronounced Russian accent. It seemed obvious to Bertie he was trying to make a move on Viv but his inexperience in the art of pickup thwarted him. He stood awkwardly at the side of her table in his tight swim-shorts and Pat Boone T-shirt. She hoped for Alex's sake that Jorge's technical research skills were an improvement on his cultural ones. Jeez, Pat Boone? Still, she felt sorry for him. Bad karma. She could have had Viv invite him to sit down, but just then, a sudden whoosh of air caught her attention. A new avatar had teleported in, all six feet of him arriving on the path right in front of the café. Above his head, a lighted symbol showed he was taken. Unlike the other avatars floating around, someone sat at his controls, someone unknown.

A confused Jorge did not look happy.

"Who the fuck are you?" He gave the newcomer a hairy eyeball, as people used to say.

She too wondered. Alex had not mentioned a second avatar. The dude looked around, took his bearings, but then his eyes alighted on Viv. He slowly lowered his sunglasses. His actions were much more skilled than any attempts Viv had made removing hers. When he undid the buckle on his jeans and stepped out of them in his red speedo, like some Mediterranean beach boy, Viv's admiration for his controller skyrocketed. Undoing a buckle was surely on a par with unravelling the Gordian knot!

"Who are you?" Jorge asked again, obviously also impressed by the avatar's dexterity.

If this wasn't one of Alex's guys, could he somehow have found a way to break into Alex's tightly controlled realm? Could he be from another company, a competitor spy?

"Don't talk to him!"

Jorge's arm shot out in front of Viv as if he feared the same thing.

"I'll talk to whomever I like," she said, surprising herself.

But Bertie felt comfortable in her second skin, which was, of course, Viv's skin. She was Viv. Nothing separated her from her avatar, and she found herself identifying as if she had never been anyone else, never Bertie, and most definitely never old. Shoving Jorge's arm away and slowly taking off Viv's glasses, though not dropping them this time, she fluttered "their" eyelashes just a tad. It proved more difficult than she expected, however, and both of Viv's eyelids clunked down, like an old-fashioned celluloid doll's.

That was the thing about becoming one. She wasn't yet consistently Viv. She oscillated between "I" and "she," between "me" and "her," mixing up pronouns as she identified with, then separated from, Viv. Swiveling back and forth in this strange new world for which she had no grammatical GPS, she kept her confusion to herself. It was like being in that presleep state when you lay there thinking and, without noticing or receiving any warning about your impending move, you slipped quietly over that liminal place into sleep. You never knew when it would happen, and it could not be forced. Sometimes, she felt she hovered between the two, unsure who she was.

"My name's Vivienne." She held out "their" bangled hand to the newcomer who introduced himself as Rick, a spot-on seventies name, she thought. When, in an exaggerated bow over "their" hand, he kissed it, she was impressed. He had something about him, that Rick. When he spoke, his voice seemed much older than Jorge's, although of course it could have been doctored just like Viv's, she thought, stepping mentally back into herself, Bertie. She admired Rick's knowledgeable controller even more and decided to call him Rick-bro.

Poor Jorge stood at a loss, not knowing what to do. If Alex found out that any of his new tweaks had been seen by an outsider, or heaven forbid stolen, he would most likely have had Jorge's hide. Bertie did not wish that on the Russian, but at the same time, Viv was not a possession to be bandied around by two competing men. Too many centuries commodifying women had left Bertie impatient with men's games. But then she thought of the new baby and how important it was for Alex to succeed in his work.

Family won out. With no warning to either man, she switched off the VR headset and the entire realm went dark. On Venice Beach, blackness wiped out ocean and beach, disappeared bathers, runners, bicyclists, and walkers, and left an absence of light in her headset. Without her, Jorge and Rick could do nothing. She was the boss of this metaverse.

●●

A cloud of uncertainty now hung over her VR world, she told Marion and Daru over quinoa, spinach, and goat cheese salad at Portage Bay Café. "He just appeared out of the blue, this Rick person, dropping out of the sky like he'd been teleporting around my realm and suddenly saw an opening. Who could he possibly be? Alex didn't say anything to me about another avatar, and the fact Jorge didn't know him either worries me."

"I hope you told Alex about him, this gate-crasher."

"What do you think? I emailed him that night, but I haven't heard back yet." She wiped vinaigrette from her lips and pushed her plate away. "It's as if Rick, or rather his controller, knew where to find us. How did he even know that a Venice Beach metaverse existed? It's not like it's advertised on some metaverse platform. It's a private creation, a construction built by Alex. Nobody knows about it except Alex, Jorge's controller, and me."

"I know about it, and Daru too."

"Yes, but neither of you would know how to enter my realm or start the program. Besides Alex, only Lisa…"

Even as she said her name, she realized. Of course! Lisa could work out how to enter Venice Beach without any problem. Bertie's VR headset lay in Lennie's study and there was nothing to stop Lisa from switching it on while she prepared food in the kitchen and set herself up as another avatar, then following through at home on her dad's headset. Her granddaughter was no spy, of course, but Bertie knew how inquisitive she could be and how savvy when it came to anything technological. She turned away so Daru and Marion could not see the concern on her face.

"Thank you." A waitress picked up her napkin, which she hadn't noticed had dropped to the floor. She gave her a new one.

By now, the restaurant had filled with customers. Around them, men and a handful of women talked loudly as they ate, no doubt gossiping about the latest hiring and firing at the big tech companies. At the next table, a young guy scribbled an equation on his napkin and showed it to his neighbor who, shaking his head, pointed out something, then scribbled over it so hard his pen pierced the paper. At the table on their other side, a couple kept their child entertained with a video game, until the waitress brought her Mickey Mouse pancake which she could then take to the fruit bar and create a face with a strawberry mouth, grape eyes, and thick curls of cream for hair.

At first, neither Daru nor Marion said anything. Then, through a mouthful of quinoa, Daru asked whether she had done anything in her metaverse that she wouldn't want Lisa to see, anything that would embarrass her, to which Bertie replied in the negative. But that didn't mean she felt comfortable having Lisa listen to Viv's words and watch what she did, and then make assumptions about her grandmother. Didn't Bertie have a right to privacy like anyone else?

"Well, I know Lisa." Marion laid her knife and fork neatly beside each other. "I am quite sure she would never do anything sneaky like that. It's just not in her nature. She adores you and would never spy on you."

Bertie held onto that thought.

● ●

When Rick appeared in her little world again the next day, she called Alex who told her not to be concerned about the new avatar; it was all under control. *His* control. She assumed then that everything must be kosher, and Rick represented no risk to the company. Certainly, Jorge seemed now to accept his presence as if he had never doubted it in the first place. Still, who was he, this person who had teleported into her realm? And why had Alex put him there? Further, was it possible that "he" could be a "she?" Her granddaughter? But why would Alex place his own daughter in Bertie's world and not inform her? There was no way she could bring herself to ask that question of her doting son-in-law. She did, however, casually quiz Lisa. Did she know how to get into her metaverse?

"Why should I want to?" Lisa looked askance at her. "Duh!"

She would rather have her own metaverse, of course. Nevertheless, Bertie proceeded nervously step by step, looking for clues even as she feared catching someone. Nothing untoward happened, however, and soon her small milieu so captivated her once again that she forgot all about her suspicions.

In this strange new world, every ordinary activity assumed new significance for Bertie, but she quickly got the hang of how things worked. A pedicure for Viv, for example, only required getting her seated and holding out her leg while some unconnected avatar moved back and forth over her feet with a minuscule varnish brush. As for the runners and walkers she crossed on the pathway, they were more than eager to engage with the lovely blonde with the vivacious smile whose bangles clattered every time she moved.

On a few occasions, surfers spoke to her about the weather, the condition of the surf, and what time the ice-cream man would do his round on the beach. When the postman delivering mail to the boxes outside the front row of houses hesitated before the pink house, Viv held out her hand, informing him, as if she lived there, that she would take its mail. By all appearances, Viv felt completely at home in this place, just as with each passing day Bertie spent on Venice Beach, her own comfort level increased. How easily she had slipped back into the texture of those times, its music, its language, and its pursuits.

Sometimes, when she peered through Viv's eyes, collisions of time ricocheted in her head. Between the present on her side of the glass and the past on Viv's side, anachronisms burst out in confusion, as if she had lost track of time. Mostly, however, they steered safely past one another, like dodgem cars, because she had become so used to that peculiar out-of-body experience of inhabiting somebody else in a different time period, of being somebody else, that she barely noticed. When Jorge and Viv chatted, Jorge gazed into "her" eyes, though they were Viv's eyes to him, and likewise, when she looked at him, it was his controller's eyes that stared back at them. Or so she thought. Who could say who saw whom? It all seemed so realistically unreal. At any one time, she could be "I," "Viv," or "she." At this early stage of her relationship with her avatar, she went in and out of existence continuously, shape-shifting and code-switching, her identity dependent on the depth of her absorption in her avatar.

Being Viv, Bertie also felt acutely aware of having a figure to die for. She wondered whether Rick-bro, whoever he was, had also felt aware of his new avatar's body, that in some strange way Rick's strong physique belonged to him too. If he were an oldster like her—there was no way to tell from his voice—he too would admire the beauty of these young people, taking note of their long limbs and firm skin, their abundance of hair, and perfect teeth.

When Bertie still worked at West Roxbury, her wards had been filled with young men recently returned from Vietnam. Though once lean and lovely, they were now disfigured, their damaged limbs a testament to war's ferocious appetite. As she nursed them back to health, their youthful skin had healed, their reset bones grown magically together again. Their muscles, atrophied from being so long bedridden, rebounded. With medical care, exercise, and rest, they were once again beautiful. She did not see their beauty, however, nor recognize the magnificence of youth, because she too was young then.

Only in retrospect, years after she moved to Vancouver, did her appreciation for their beauty emerge. At Vancouver General, where she had landed a job in gerontology, the patients under her care ranged in age from sixty to ninety. There were no more gorgeous people, only overweight elderly men whose beer bellies required lifting separately from their bodies when she tried to turn them. Horny toenails, thinning hair, rickety knees, skin tags and bumps, sagging breasts, and veined, arthritic hands... that was what greeted her every day. None of it was reversible no matter how much she coaxed and goaded. As ashamed as she was to admit it, even though she cared uncomplainingly and, she hoped, tenderly with her patients' decrepitude, she found no beauty in it. It was simply something she preferred not to look at. That is, until one day it hit her that she was it; she was decrepit. All the time she had been in thrall to Arielle's graduation and marriage, then Lennie's new position with the governor, the years had sped by, and now she too had rickety knees and arthritic hands.

When she, Marion, and Daru got together, they often joked about their physical and mental degeneration, eliciting guffaws from one another for their widening waists and flattened bums, for their lost collagen that no moisturizer could replace. But, of course, such talk lost its self-deprecatory humor when outsiders listened. Sometimes she wondered why they couldn't maintain the illusion, along with Jane Fonda and Mary Steenburgen, that age was all fun and games.

"Why can't I pretend the person I see in the mirror when I hold in my stomach and turn the more flattering side of my face forward, and dim the lights, is the one others see?" Marion once asked. "And not the woman with the dowager's hump and rounded shoulders rushing to the store to buy her constipation pills?"

"Enough!" Daru would sometimes shout when they went at it too long in this vein. Truth is a downer; and that's the truth.

# CHAPTER 12

———

"DON'T YOU THINK IT'S IRONIC?" MARION SAID AS THEY strolled back to the apartment.

Daru had gone her own way, as she needed to pick up her groceries first, having promised to make them a tandoori meal which required marinating the chicken in yogurt and tandoor spices overnight. They would share the chicken with rice, lemon, and onions for lunch tomorrow.

"What's ironic?"

"I thought you hated how age made you invisible."

"I do. Don't you?"

"Sure. Yet, you love hiding out of sight behind Viv and being invisible. Like an observer."

"I would say I was a bit more than an observer," Bertie retorted. "After all, Viv doesn't exist without me. She can't move a finger or speak."

Standing at the curb waiting to cross Westlake Avenue, she looked right, then left, as if she planned to make a dash for it across two lanes of traffic. Their police no longer ticketed jaywalkers, like they did before Defund the Police.

"Yes, but nobody sees you, do they? Nobody notices you," she rubbed it in to make sure Bertie had understood her point and that she'd won.

Sometimes Bertie thought retirement had made the three of them more competitive than if nursing, law, and television still occupied their time. Weren't they supposed to grow more mellow with age?

Next to her, an impatient young man bashed the traffic light arrow with the side of his fist. In their neighborhood, speed was of the essence, but for all the man's bashing, he could not make the light change faster. He had to wait.

Marion, of course, had it right on invisibility. Bertie's positions were indeed contradictory, and inconsistent. But wasn't inconsistency a prerogative when you reached their age? That's what she wanted to argue, but she knew it would not hold weight. Still, she could think of no other riposte. Invisibility had just not occurred to her in the context of the metaverse, even though it had come up in earlier days when Marion, testing her cultural antennae, had suggested creating an avatar of color. After all, nobody could see her. Who would know she was white?

Being so engaged with Viv—moving her body, speaking for her—Bertie had thought of the two of them as one and therefore visible to Jorge and Rick. To Rick-bro, however, she was invisible. He saw only Viv.

"Voyeurism, that's what it is, Old Bean. That's how you're getting your kicks," Marion went on. "You can't deny it."

"It's possible to be actor and observer at the exact same time, Old Carrot," she said, one-upping her, though she wasn't sure Marion fully understood what her position felt like.

She wasn't certain what it felt like herself. Sometimes, an image from *The Handmaid's Tale* of husband, wife, and handmaid intertwined in bed, simulating, pretending that what was happening wasn't, would flit through her mind and she imagined herself sitting on Viv's shoulders, being her, replacing her, all the while sprouting soothing words to make the denial easier. It was a disturbing image; one she had no intention of sharing with Marion.

"Old Carrot" took Bertie's reference in stride and flaunted her dyed mane, shaking it out next to her like a wet dog. As they walked into the lobby of Mariela Plaza, each feeling she had gained a point, she linked her arm through Bertie's, and they shuffled in like two mischievous schoolgirls. From the smile on the new concierge's face as they headed for the elevator, he probably judged them drunk.

# CHAPTER 13

———

"I WANT TO MARRY SOMEONE LIKE GRAMPS," LISA announced as they strolled through the vegetable aisles at Whole Foods on Westlake Avenue. The locals, who were mostly men, crowded around the ready-made wraps and rotisserie chickens, the single-serving lasagnas, and packaged tortillas. Most nights, those products suited her too, but with Lisa in tow, she made a show of buying fresh fruits and vegetables, promising her they would vitalize her hair and skin. But Lisa's mind lay elsewhere.

"I don't want to marry someone like Dad."

"Your dad is a terrific guy and a great father."

"Yeah, but he only talks about technical stuff. I want someone—I mean, I may never marry, of course, but if I did—I want someone who talks about people and feelings, like Grandpa did."

"You know, talk is only part of life. You also must be responsible for practical things like paying bills and fixing the leaky faucet."

But Lisa apparently had her mind made up.

"I want a marriage like you and Gramps had...at least, before he died."

She scowled at Bertie disapprovingly. She hadn't forgotten her verbal perfidy and had already reminded her of it three times in the last week. Even so, the marriage itself still registered in Lisa's mind as sacrosanct, a state of eternal happiness that she wanted for herself. Bertie felt flattered, but at the same time, needed to disabuse her of the notion that angels had catered their wedding.

"Nobody's perfect, you know, not even Grandpa."

When Lisa's eyebrows inched closer together and her lips pouched ready to retort, she backpedaled.

"Though I must admit, he was a pretty good husband. Even when we argued and I screamed at him, he never shouted back. He always disagreed calmly and said things like, 'point taken' or else, 'I understand why it might seem that way to you.'"

"See, that's the way it should be, not like Mom and Dad who mutter, 'What do you know about medicine?' Or 'You are so ignorant about technology.'"

If only Lennie had screamed and shouted, Bertie thought. Instead, he hid behind words like a psychoanalyst, using them to edge her where she did not want to go. She could still hear those strategically chosen words worming their way through her mind, nudging her forward, flattering her—"How do you feel about that?" "Do you think you might be...?" "When you were a child, did you...?"—until she agreed, yes, he hadn't flirted with his colleague from the governor's office, or the woman author he interviewed for the article on education, or the ex-girlfriend who still had a thing for him.

"Sometimes, you know, even your gramps could do and say things that drove me up the wall."

"That was probably just the antagonist inside you. Gramps never said anything I didn't like."

Her angelic, adoring smile would have gladdened Lennie's heart. He loved female smiles directed at him. He loved females, period; loved being around them, talking to them, listening to them. Most of the time, Bertie could handle it. She knew somewhere deep inside that Lennie was committed to her, and needed her in some way she didn't quite understand. Maybe if he had bought a convertible in his late forties, or revived a long-standing passion for drawing, or raising horses, or climbing mountains, they might have avoided the tsunami that eventually hit them.

Busy attending night classes to advance her nursing career, she didn't see the telltale signs...the sudden fastidiousness about his dress, the late-night "office" calls, and the time she found a tube of lipstick in his jacket pocket which he claimed belonged to a colleague who, not wanting to carry a purse into a board meeting, asked if he'd mind holding onto it until later.

As for her own crisis, after her years nursing Vietnam vets back to health, the elderly patients at Vancouver General had gradually worn her down. She longed to escape these Canadian geriatrics with their old people problems that seemed suddenly to stick to her like cobwebs. One day much too soon, she feared she too would complain about constipation and bemoan the loss of her brain cells.

The day the tsunami hit, she had spent the morning dealing with chronic coughs, high blood pressure, flatulence, and stiffening joints. Knowing now at seventy-five what it felt like to have old-age aches and pains that interfered with her life, she should of course have been more compassionate with her patients. But all she wanted was to flee to her 6:00 p.m. class at Vancouver Coastal Health on Broadway where she would interact with enthusiastic young people with inquisitive minds and hopes for the future. *Oh, the hypocrisy of it all!* But what could she say? During her last three months taking the class, the nursing students' energy and curiosity had rejuvenated her and proved the perfect antidote to her fears about aging.

Even as she stepped into the Coastal Health lobby that day in 1989 when she was just forty-two, her spirits had lifted, and she took the stairs two at a time. When she arrived, however, she found their classroom empty. Affixed to the door, a sign read "Canceled until next week." Feeling disappointed, she nevertheless joined a group of fellow students for a drink at a local bar, eventually making her way back home just before seven.

In the summer months in Vancouver, nature only pulled the plug on daylight at about 9:00 p.m. Kids still kicked ball in the street, and smoke drifted over the fence smelling of fatty sausages and hamburger meat. Arielle slept at her friend Jolene's house, and Lennie said he would be out late interviewing a woman suspected of leaking highly secret government letters to a newspaper in China. Feeling a little woozy having drunk on an empty stomach, Bertie wanted to lie down for a while before getting herself something to eat. So, she kicked off her shoes and left them at the bottom of the stairs as she usually did. Then she headed in the direction of their bedroom, holding the rail for support.

The house heaved and sighed beneath her feet, as if it too felt woozy. Sunlight wavered through the upper hallway window catching the dancing dust motes that her heels disturbed, and she felt like she was moving through a dreamlike fantasy. It made her sleepy and she wondered whether she needed a proper nap rather than a lie-down. In this state, she wasn't ready for the sight that hijacked her breath, not that one could ever be ready for shock, no matter how well prepared. She wondered if she was drunk. Could two beers have been enough to distort her vision?

Through the floating, whirling specks of dust, the strange shape emerged, hazy at first. As she stepped up to the doorway, she blinked her eyes twice at the monstrosity on their bed and the ghoul grew clearer. No humpbacked monster this, but a buck-naked woman crouched over a trouser-less Lennie, who lay flat on his back, his hands pressing on her shoulders, his mouth open, but for once not talking. Whoever she was, this person who had suddenly intruded into their lives, her dark hair hung down on either side of her face and created a private space over Lennie's body, from which Bertie could hear the sucking, slurping sounds that broadcast her action. Bertie must have gasped or made some sound because both their heads shot up, creating a tableau of horror that left a stomach-turning image etched in her brain.

Nothing prepares a woman for betrayal. There are no right words, no perfect response to this new knowledge. She threatened divorce and threw Lennie out, but three months later, after he implored her to forgive him, after her pain had receded to a dull ache, she took him back. Yes, she knew. But women do that—men too—because it is hard to jettison a relationship which contains so much of your history and identity, and into which you have poured your emotional capital. Lennie was contrite, swearing this had been the only time he'd strayed. Did she believe him? Maybe. Or maybe she just wasn't strong enough to fight against the undertow of his words that washed her back to the familiar shore.

# CHAPTER 14

---

THE NEXT WEEK, BERTIE SPENT AT LEAST A COUPLE OF hours each day trying to perfect Viv's small motor skills. Each of her actions—combing her hair, pulling coins out of her purse—took numerous repetitions. At least her large bag had a wide mouth, so she didn't need to deal with zips that got stuck. The comb too came with an excellent grip that fit right into Viv's hand.

It wasn't only the physical aspects of Viv's life that engaged her. Bertie soon realized this avatar she refined also needed a life history to place her in the world and to imbue her with the immaterial heft that would account for what she said and did. Sure, Bertie could make up facts as they were needed in conversation, but she wanted to be better prepared so Viv never ended up in an awkward situation sprouting contradictory things about herself.

Her first inkling of who Viv might be came from the sound of her voice. Yes, she knew it was her own voice contorted by AI modulations, but she had to identify what it would sound like to other people. It was certainly Californian, but by no means could you say it originated in Los Angeles. No, this was a small-town girl from somewhere inland, perhaps San Leandro, Indio, or Merced—she made it Merced—who had moved to LA in search of excitement and opportunities. Maybe she'd had it with the boring administrative job at Castle Air Force Base that she'd held ever since high school. In her imagination, being surrounded by dashing men in uniform who at any point might be called away to global trouble spots had sounded thrilling, but she'd soon discovered that only in movies were pilots more interesting than accountants or almond farmers. Besides, most days she'd handled the oil-splattered paperwork of mechanics.

With each new fact Bertie made up about Viv, she understood her better. She wanted to know more, so even as she emptied the dishwasher now, she continued to create further details about her story. Sometimes she would second-guess herself or create alternatives that she couldn't decide between. She felt something more must have persuaded Viv to make the break from Merced and her family, but she didn't know what. She was still working it out. Could it have been something to do with an older brother? Chris? Will?

A thriving heroin industry kept many of Merced's young people addicted, and Chris had proved no exception. He probably would have kept his addiction hidden from their parents, maintaining the straight, polite demeanor they expected—their father sat on the city council and demanded his children never behave in a way that might embarrass him in front of his colleagues—but Viv knew what Chris got up to in his room. She knew too how ugly he could become when he reached empty and a refuel lay not in timely reach. Still, she loved her brother, and seeing him sink into the depths of uncontrollable need left her feeling helpless. She wanted him to stop but knew he couldn't. How many times had she seen him stashing syringes and needles under the pile of shirts in his bedroom?

Just then, the "radar" ringtone on Bertie's phone abruptly pulled her back from 1970s Merced into the present.

"Mrs. Glazer, this is Bernadette from Dr. Meredith's office. You missed your appointment with the doctor."

"My appointment isn't until the fourteenth."

"The fourteenth was two days ago, Mrs. Glazer."

Now she would have to wait weeks before Meredith could check out that strange mole on her leg that she could swear had grown since she last looked. Between her and Marion, they had at least eight ex-moles that now merely resembled blemishes that fortunately you could cover up with a bit of cream.

"I am really sorry, Bernadette. I don't know how I missed it. Usually, I am so careful about writing things down on my calendar. Is there any chance you can get me another appointment?"

Luckily, someone had cancelled their appointment for next week, so Bernadette scheduled her for that Wednesday.

"Should I send you a reminder? A lot of our older patients like to receive a text reminder."

Nasty woman! There was no way she wanted a text reminder.

Bernadette was just another distraction in her day. She had already been on the phone to a plumber because the toilet wouldn't stop flushing, and the bakery that she called to deliver raisin-cinnamon bagels for Lisa so she didn't have to go to the store herself had messed up the order, and she now had a dozen poppy seed bagels which she doubted her granddaughter would eat. She would have to freeze them.

All she wanted was to get back to Venice Beach so she could let Viv have some fun. It's not like she had all the time in the world to hang out there. For one thing, the mornings were out, as she'd discovered soon after parading Viv when they first met. Nobody turned up at the beach before having slept off the effects of their previous night's indulgences, which meant they didn't arrive until noon. She supposed, if her new parallel world had been in the Pacific Northwest where the summer sun hung around till 9:00 or 10:00 p.m., she could have continued having fun with Viv and Rick till late into the night. But in California, the sun retired early, having exhausted itself after working so hard at projecting its brilliance. As a result, she couldn't see anything. No streetlights lit the beach, and besides, she couldn't wear her glasses inside the VR headset.

Yesterday, just as she readied herself to put on the headset, Daru arrived at the apartment. Would she go with her to Lindstrom? She had donated all her old clothes to Goodwill because the time had come to start her new life, and she needed a fresh wardrobe to go with it.

"That's wonderful, Daru," Bertie congratulated her, though to be honest, she was amazed at her sudden turnaround.

Two years after Lennie's death, here *she* was still wearing her old khakis from L.L.Bean and her favorite long white linen shirt. But, anyway, good for Daru. She was delighted her friend was making this effort.

"But could we go tomorrow instead?" She procrastinated, which is why the two of them ended up this morning in the downtown store looking at clothes designed for 20-year-olds.

Nobody had ever told them to move to the old lady section; that was for other women, not them. Whatever their bodies looked like on the outside, in their heads they remained the same as they had always been. They headed for the type of clothes that had flattered them best when they were young, in Bertie's case the long silky shirts that flowed with her body then, but now stretched tight around her belly.

Alongside them, young women tried on pants cut off at an unattractive angle to their ankles, and tops that bared their midriffs. The new fashion flared pants, so like bell-bottoms, could have been a possibility for her and Daru, except they needed to be matched with tight tops tucked in with a belt. Even when seventies fashions returned in modern form, they were purposely designed to make it impossible for reruns by oldsters like them. In the end, it didn't matter. The saleswomen on the floor ignored them; they were invisible. So, when they tired of waiting to be served, they uploaded their irritation to the cloud, and just left. Bertie never bought her shirt.

At the shoe department, however, a young man attended to them after they had waved the shoe Daru wanted right under his nose. Finally, some attention! They sat down to wait for him to bring her size thirty-nine, not unhappy to take the weight off their feet. Around them, young girls wobbled by on glitzy, strappy heels, then stopped to admire their legs in the long mirrors angled backward to project the most flattering image. Where could they possibly go in such shoes? Bertie wondered. They would be impossible to dance in.

"Here we are." The salesman pulled up one of those seats with the rubber-coated strut on which the customer places her foot. He sat down, sidewise, she noticed, perhaps so as not to end up with the customer's foot between his thighs. Lifting the lid off the shoebox, he checked with Daru that the shoe inside was indeed the one she wanted—a soft, black suede that looked perfect for Daru, both comfy and fashionable. But then, he raised her leg onto the strut, indicating for her to take off her sock and Bertie sensed Daru hesitate. Did she have a hole in her sock? Could she not reach her foot? Bertie bent over to help, but Daru pushed her hand aside. Skirting the edge between self-confidence and doubt, she rolled the sock down herself. When it finally came off, and the salesman's eyes landed on her bunion and disfigured toenails, he instantly recoiled.

"I used to be a runner; messed up my nails years ago," Daru apologized.

The salesman tried to catch himself, but it was too late. They had both seen his expression of disgust. Oh, the indignity of it all!

●●

To compensate for the morning's bruising, they had lunch at the restaurant and indulged themselves with a good bottle of sauvignon.

To raise Daru's spirits further, when they returned to the apartment, Bertie offered her a peek into her metaverse.

"Come into my lab," she said, inviting her with an exaggerated bow, after first securing her promise never to mention this time-capsuled world to anyone.

For the last month or two, Bertie had enthusiastically described what she saw through the headset, but to Daru, it had all seemed fantastical. How could a simulation be as realistic as the real thing.

"Wait until you've seen it before you pass judgment," Bertie said.

She handed her the headset and told her to take off her glasses. Alex hadn't yet worked out what to do with those, though you would think it a priority, given how many people wore them. It turned out the challenge had something to do with the amount of space inside the headset and how many pounds it could bear before it weighed down the wearer.

"Good grief!" Daru parroted Peanuts and grabbed her arm for balance. "I feel like I'm in the middle of a storm."

Bertie held onto her while she turned her head this way and that. She wouldn't let Daru touch the controllers, so she saw only the set scenery and a stationary Viv in her side mirror. She couldn't move anyone.

"Viv reminds me so much of what's-her-name's cousin," she said.

"Who?"

"You know, the one with the blonde hair who likes to wear embroidered, puffy tops."

"You mean Lesley from our book club?"

"No, no, the one who works in advertising."

"Oh, that one. Begins with a *P*."

"Right!"

"What's her name again?"

They never remembered "P's" name, but the whole scenario Daru had seen while wearing the VR headset impressed her. She couldn't stop talking about how realistic everything appeared on the screen.

"I could even smell the coconut oil."

"Sure!" Bertie laughed, knowing that replicating the sense of smell with the headset was impossible.

Alex had told her that creating smell in the metaverse still lay beyond anyone's algorithmic capabilities, but perhaps it was the power of suggestion that after Daru left and she replaced the VR headset on her head, she smelled it too, a definite whiff of coconut oil. She zeroed in on a young man who appeared to be rubbing tanning oil onto the thighs of a bikini-clad woman, but close up, the smell disappeared. For a moment, she'd believed Alex was pulling out all the stops. What next? Could he mimic the smell of pot from the funky T-shirt store where they used to buy their stash? But no, there was no smell of coconut, only the mental memory of it from some long-ago day on a real beach.

Marion had also tried out the headset a week before but, unlike Daru, she had pronounced the whole experience creepy.

"Cognitive dissonance," she had growled, merging the two realities as she came out of the digital one, exclaiming, "Where am I?"

Bertie had left Viv's connection live but warned Marion as she had Daru not to touch anything. Marion, however, just could not resist.

"Viv imitated everything I did," she said, amazed, but obviously disturbed by the mirror experience. "It was bizarre. If I pushed out my stomach far enough, she did too, and if I stuck out my tongue…"

"You didn't!"

"I was just playing around to see how far she would go. I swear, if I'd farted, she would have done so too!"

"When I think of the amount of damage you could have done to Viv's relationship with Rick, Marion…" she lashed out, denying the possessive tendrils tightening around her heart at the thought of Viv responding to Marion's actions like she did with her. If only she could explain to Rick-bro that it wasn't her clowning around like that. She would hate him to think her a fool. Whoever he was.

"Then why didn't you tell me that Viv would copy everything I did?" Marion defended herself.

"Because, dude, I didn't think you would touch the buttons that I asked you not to touch!"

"Dude?" She cocked her head. "As far as I know, we are not living in 1974! Anyway, I don't like it, this avatar business. It was like having a mini-me ready to do my urging, ready to act out all my thoughts and especially my mess-ups. Besides, it's so…so…" She twisted a section of her red hair behind her ear. "It's like you're living in someone else's fun in the sun. And not even a real person's."

"And how is that different from reading a light novel and vicariously living the character's fun-in-the-sun adventure? Same with escapist movies? Don't you dig watching an actor's pleasure, especially if you identify with her in some way? In fact," she said, even as Marion winced at her use of the word "dig," "what I'm doing constitutes a step up from books and movies because I am *creating* the character I'm enjoying."

"But surely that's worse, not better!" She pitched one of her Marion looks, as if to say "Duh!"

They all had their ways of being dismissive. If it had been Daru, she would simply have ignored Marion's words, pretended she hadn't heard anything so she could avoid a response. Sort of passive-aggressive, Bertie had always thought, but also effective. For her part, she just threw up her hands. Some things were not worth saying.

Marion eventually left, giving her a chummy hug, and muttering about it being hard enough to live in this world. Why on earth did she need another one with its own set of challenges?

# CHAPTER 15

---

SHE WAS PLEASED FINALLY TO BE BACK ON HER OWN AT Venice Beach. The same NPCs walked the beach or pumped their muscles, but to one side, someone had erected a volleyball net and two teams of suntanned girls smashed the ball back and forth. Being unlive but programmed, the leggy volleyballers with their repetitive actions soon became boring, their minimal conversation a litany of "good save!" "sorry!" "get it!"

Their game did not attract Rick's attention. He and Jorge remained stuck where Bertie had left them. Instead of returning to their controllers—maybe she should have switched off the machine more gradually when she closed things down, as you do a computer, thus crossing wires with the other two avatars—the two of them hovered there with Viv in anticipation of their next adventures. Unlike empty puppets waiting for the hand that pulls the strings, however, they stood upright, nonchalantly looking around as if there were nowhere else they wanted to be.

As soon as Viv turned her head, however, Jorge lit up. The guy must have had an alert to warn him when she reopened, for he immediately began talking to Viv and asking questions, but when she answered in Spanglish, he looked lost.

"Oh, I thought..." she began in her Merced accent.

Latinos formed a major part of the Merced population so everyone knew at least some Spanish, but in Jorge's case, perhaps Russian would have been the better option. Exposed in his cultural disguise, Jorge appeared momentarily lost. He muttered something that sounded to Bertie like *chert*, causing Viv to revert to English, explaining she attended community college and this was her second year. Not a lie exactly, but something Bertie hadn't yet included in the biography she'd patched together earlier.

Her answer, though hers, of course, made it seem that Viv had claimed her life for herself. Bertie had been reading lately about bots—AI—that upgraded their skills as they learned. Thus they grew more human with each development. Algorithms were beyond her, but surely it wasn't possible to bring an avatar to life unless it had been programmed to do that from the beginning. Viv was just a simple avatar that Alex had created to her specifications, right?

To make Jorge's situation even more awkward, another bit of Viv's biography inserted itself unexpectedly. As she crossed her leg, her sandal caught the plunger part of a discarded syringe, its needle not fully retracted so the sharp end with its contaminating point stuck out threateningly. A cascade of Bertie's memories inserting needles into patients' arms, buttocks, and thighs clashed disconcertingly with recollections that simultaneously took her back into Viv's family home in Merced. Caught between the two, she vacillated, but at that point, she embodied Viv more than she did herself, so she shook "her" foot hard, and when that did not dislodge the syringe, she hyperventilated and shouted to Jorge, "Get it away from me!" It caused the poor man to flounder and become all fingers. Removing the syringe without pricking himself or Viv lay beyond him. She had pushed Viv's foot as far from her body as possible. A quick look in the side-view mirror showed the syringe dangling midair from Viv's sandal, close to Jorge's face. When he shouted for her to lift her toes where the plunger handle caught, she stared blankly.

"Lift them, damn it!" (What? Did he think she was a magician and could lift Viv's toes? Her manipulations had improved fantastically, but to lift her toes separate from her foot?) When she still hesitated, Jorge gingerly pushed up the big toe with one finger, showing off his own controller's deftness, which caused the syringe to clatter to the ground. Even fifteen minutes later, despite Jorge's assurances that he'd disposed of it, she still shivered, seeing in it every needle her brother had plunged into himself.

Moving in and out of Viv's skin gave Bertie psychological whiplash. For her own equilibrium she tried to hold onto Bertie's identity, but she found the boundary between them so porous that she would slip over without even realizing she no longer stood on her side, the real side. Again, she was reminded of falling asleep, the moment of passing from consciousness to sleep unnoticed, keeping her unaware until she slipped soundlessly over the threshold. Perhaps, sleepwalking came closest to the out-of-body/in-body experience she was living.

The enigmatic Rick missed the entire scene with Jorge and the syringe. While his body remained present, his person must have been AWOL. Where was he all that time? Wasn't his controller supposed to be keeping tabs on them? But perhaps she misunderstood and had the relationship all wrong. She didn't grasp who Rick was. Maybe he was a spy after all. When he finally became live, he looked around as if reacquainting himself with his whereabouts. Then he folded his threads into the colorful macramé sling bag over his shoulder and tightened the rubber band around his long, sun-bleached hair. She could see his entire musculature in action, biceps bulging. That Rick-bro knew what he was doing with Rick. Damn, he was good.

"Well, see you later." Jorge wandered off, a beach flaneur.

Fuck. Last week he was bugged out about Rick and today he couldn't care less if he were a spy and could steal Alex's ideas. No doubt Alex had told him not to bother, but had he explained why Rick was no longer a concern? Did Jorge know more than she did about Rick? He certainly didn't seem bothered by Rick's presence, as if he didn't consider him a danger anymore.

Had the competition for Viv's attention just proved more than Jorge could take, so he'd decided to step away? It was obvious Elvis Presley had arrived on Venice Beach in his blue suede shoes and Pat Boone didn't stand a chance. She noticed Jorge wore a new T-shirt today, one that read "The day the music died"; Buddy Holly was definitely a step up from Boone musically, if not chronologically. When would someone at Alex's office enlighten Jorge and encourage him to update his T-shirt icons from the fifties to the seventies?

While she mused on this recent development, Rick had been talking to, or rather at, Viv, who during Bertie's lapse of attention appeared strapped for words. Her silence hadn't discouraged him, however, for now he leaned on her table and asked whether he could chill with her. She patted the seat beside her, and he draped himself across it, spreading his legs, or rather manspreading, as people say today. There was barely any hair on his body, and he had the beautiful golden tan of someone blonde. On his feet, he wore the ubiquitous blue flip-flops. He was not Bertie's type in the metaverse, nor would he have been in the seventies. Nevertheless, she saw what Viv might find appealing about him. After all, she was not talking marriage for

Viv, just innocent romance like she'd had back then with that drummer who busked on Ocean Front Walk and greeted her with "Hey, sunshine," and told her she was "out of sight." He had a shaggin' wagon parked up the street.

For conversation, Rick turned out to be no Lennie, but he had charisma. "And did you really..." She leaned forward as if she found his words scintillating. Turned out he was a student at UCLA majoring in psychology. She expected a Psych 101 discussion of the id from lover boy, but his talk of the unconscious went straight to dreams, a subject Bertie remembered having fascinated her too in the days when pot could give you the most bizarre ones.

She and Lennie would decipher each other's nighttime ramblings, having great fun picking out the anomalies and skewed ideas to make sense of them. His dreams were vivid, and he had the knack of remembering them the next morning. More often than not, they were anxiety dreams in which he arrived in some Canadian town to give a speech, only to realize he had prepared the wrong speech. Or, he'd turned up in the incorrect town, and found the doors closed, with nobody expecting him at all.

Rick was obviously stoked by what he had learned in his class on the illusions and delusions of the mind. He was hoping to keep the conversation going so he could show Viv what he knew.

"So, what was your funkiest dream ever?" he asked her.

Toggling the red switch, Bertie peeped at Viv in her side mirror and saw her making a show of thinking. She leaned back in the chair, her arms behind her head so her breasts rode up, drawing his eyes toward them. Bertie wasn't purposely trying to make Viv seductive, although given their talk of the unconscious, maybe she was. In truth, she just needed extra time to think of a response. She filched a dream of her own, which if not exactly funky, certainly had intrigued her at the time.

"There is one that sort of freaked me out," she confessed to Rick, who told her to lay it on him.

"See," she began hesitantly, unsure whether her dream would pass muster with someone in his twenties, "it happened at a fairground among roller coasters, dive bombers, swings that fly out like a skirt...that kind of thing."

"You went on one of those?'

"No, though any of them would have been less creepy than what I actually rode." She leaned forward and fixed her eyes, which were Bertie's eyes, on his, as if they were sharing an intimacy, which in a way she was, because what could be more personal than a dream, what more transparent of one's vulnerabilities. "No, it was something quite different." She smiled with what Bertie hoped looked like intrigue. "Not what you would expect at all. Do you know those drum things that spin you around with such centrifugal force that you stick to the walls suspended?"

"And the floor falls away below your feet? Yeah," he encouraged her, "rotors."

"Except, my dream rotor was *not* like an ordinary rotor."

Immersed in her story now, elbows on the table, Viv explained that when this rotor sped up, instead of forcing her against the wall centrifugally, it flung her back and forth. "It was like being in a destructive tornado that had made up its mind to pulverize me. I had no idea what was happening except that I hurt something awful and couldn't stop the drum from spinning. Only when the bumpy ride ended and I stepped outside, did I realize the rotor hadn't turned me into a pile of dust, but instead had chipped away at my angularities. Anything even remotely uneven or unsightly was gone."

"Far out!"

"Like a stone ground in a spinner, I had been worn smooth and shiny."

Though the meaning of the dream seemed obvious to Bertie, Rick made a show of thinking, which made her wonder if Rick-bro could be one of these purely rational types who couldn't interpret anything that wasn't black-and-white, zero and one. Finally, however, he came up with his analysis.

"Well, it's clear to me you're a free spirit, Viv, and society is trying to shape you into someone who conforms to its rules." Rick looked proud of his interpretation, but he wasn't done. With his face turned toward them and looking into their eyes, he touched his hand to their exposed knee, whispering, "Listen, Vivienne, don't ever give in to the man. You hear me? It's what the old suits want in this country, to have us shaped like little peas in a pod, so they can categorize and control us."

It was so easy to mock Rick's sincerity, but they had all felt like that in the sixties and seventies, believing the government was capable of any atrocity that increased its power. With the Orange Man sniffing around the edges of the central government wanting in, they were thankful "their man" held the reins of power.

In Bertie's little meta-realm, however, she was "the man." Rick-bro and she, when they weren't themselves Rick and Viv, were the puppeteers controlling the action in their digital world, and Rick-bro had made the first move. Her eyes rested on Rick's hand on Viv's knee. The fun had begun. Good. She liked the vibes between Viv and Rick. Between her and Rick-bro too.

# CHAPTER 16

—

"WE ARE OUT OF BAGELS!" LISA SHOOK BERTIE'S ARM, JOLT-
ing her off Venice Beach, her feet still covered in sand.

Though her real feet remained in their usual stance, planted
on the floor of Lennie's study three feet apart for balance, Lisa's
jolt almost dislodged them, obliging Bertie to latch onto the
back of the chair to stay upright. Switching off virtual reality,
she removed the headset, then blinked blindly at the change
in light. She hadn't heard Lisa come in, engrossed as she was
in her metaverse where she was trying to bend Viv at the waist
and lift her leg at the same time, as if her avatar were taking
off her pants and stepping into her bikini. The movement had
proved more of a challenge than she'd expected. Given her own
difficulty standing on one leg, they still had a long way to go.
With the utmost care, Bertie placed the headset in its special
resting place on a cushion on Lennie's desk. Once Sarssein put
it on the market, the thing would retail at a couple of thousand,
Alex had informed her, so she wasn't about to treat it like a
baseball hat. At that price, though, she didn't see it being the
next chicken in every pot.

"Did you forget about my bagels because your antagonist has been pushing you around?"

Lisa frowned at her over the missing bagels, those secular icons of what remained of Jewish life. Her wrinkled brow reminded Bertie of Arielle's when her daughter held back criticism. Though she had never said it in so many words, Arielle wished Bertie had been more like Alex's mother, Leah, a *bubbe* who, until her death nine years ago, had swaddled her grandchild in adoration and homemade cookies with sprinkles. But while Bertie loved Lisa as much as Leah did, she and her granddaughter had a different relationship, one that she liked to believe allowed them both to grow. And who didn't want to grow, even at the age of seventy-five? Certainly, anyone who survived the disappointments and unfulfilled ambitions of seventy-five years of living would jump at the chance to become a brighter, kinder, or deeper person. For, no matter how you retrospectively edit the journey of your life, you know very well where you have fallen short.

Bertie was obviously still falling short. She checked the cupboards, hoping to find an errant bagel she might have misplaced when distracted. She often did that sort of thing if her thoughts lay elsewhere, days later finding an apple in the bathroom closet or the toothpaste in the fridge, wondering how they had got there. From the medical pundits, however, she learned that such mishaps didn't necessarily signal Alzheimer's. Even youngish people did it on occasion.

"It's that antagonist of yours that's creating problems for everyone." Lisa stood in front of her with arms crossed, like a small taskmaster.

"Everyone?" It turned out that Marion and Daru were fed up with her too. She never returned their phone calls.

"You need to get it under control, Gran. Show your antagonist who's the boss, otherwise we are all going to be mad at you. Daru told me yesterday at some stage you must have internalized it—I'm going to call it B2, Bertie 2—because of some disturbing incident, and now B2 is fully ensconced, and you don't even know when it's playing you."

That Daru and Lisa had been discussing her concerned Bertie more than Daru's psychological interpretation. She felt transparent under her granddaughter's gaze. Lisa had turned the tables, and Bertie squirmed like one of the characters in her video games, when in truth she had no objection to B2 whose antagonistic grist to her more easygoing mill kept her on her toes. Who wanted to be Ms. Agreeable, when with a bit of a push you could steer yourself and your friends to further heights?

"Ta-da!" She held a hard-as-rock bagel under Lisa's nose. "All that fuss and it was just there, at the back of the fridge between the tamari and ketchup. Once I put it in the oven, it will taste as good as fresh. You'll see."

"Gran, it's not even cinnamon and raisin."

Every Friday night at their family dinner, Bertie gave Alex a short recap of her experience using the headset. She told him what actions worked well for her or where she wished certain functions could be improved or made more user-friendly. Keeping her report strictly to the working of the product, she avoided discussing what actually happened on Venice Beach except where it impinged on her explanation of a particular problem. She also never recounted Viv and Rick's conversations. She had no wish to share with the family what went on in her private metaverse. Then, one time, in her enthusiasm for getting across a point about the mechanical awkwardness of uncrossing a knee, she got carried away.

"And so, my left leg was crossed over my right knee, and I was telling Rick my dream about the fairground," she informed Alex, "and how this rotor flung me back and forth..."

"The rotor flung *you*?"

"Yes. That's what I said."

Alex was interrupting her story. Why didn't he listen more carefully?

"And while Rick was empathizing with me," she continued, "and explaining what the dream probably meant—he'd had some psych class and thought he understood its significance—he leaned over, and he touched my leg."

"*Your* leg?" Alex grinned.

"What?"

"Congratulations!" He raised his wine glass and smiled at her like a proud teacher whose student had passed the test. "You're living the simulation, Bertie."

"Gran, you did it. You've become Viv!" Lisa high-fived her, though her enthusiasm didn't quite match her father's.

"I hope Viv didn't object to Rick touching your knee instead of hers."

At that, Arielle burst out laughing, so Bertie felt like the child in the family who had missed what was obvious to everyone else. At the same time, a sense of accomplishment settled over her. For what, she wasn't exactly sure—that she had merged her identity into Viv's or Viv's into hers? That she had stepped over the barrier between the real world and taken up residency in the unreal without even realizing it? That she had shown herself capable of straddling both worlds? Whatever. She raised her glass and drank to her avatar who had brought her to this point. She had become part of the new technology, a player who could hold her own at seventy-five.

As it happened, the incident with Rick did not end there. Although Bertie never shared this part of the story with Alex, when Rick touched his hand to Viv's leg, he immediately noticed the raised scar just above her left knee.

"What happened here?" He ran his finger over the ridges. Keloid tissue had built up like a mountain range, even though no other scar on her body had ever hardened in that way. Even the sun had not lightened its rough effect.

In her specifications to Alex, Bertie had requested he code Viv a scar, but having procrastinated about Viv's back story for this identifying mark, she now found herself in the hot seat having to think up something convincing on the fly. What if...? No, that wouldn't work. Too predictable. Then, perhaps...no, too cheesy.

At West Roxbury, she would often make up stories. Then, they involved damaged young men who lay on their wards wrestling their personal monsters. The nurses all did it to see their struggling patients as people with histories that inspired their compassion and empathy. Otherwise, they were mere body parts, broken pieces, and damaged organs the nurses would handle like meat. People suffered burnout in the seventies too, just like the Covid nurses experienced while facing one case after another of upturned faces with blue lips struggling to breathe with mechanical ventilation. When the numbers reached the thousands, they stopped counting.

But Viv's story...Rick still rubbed her scar while Viv waited for words to spout from her lips. Quick, Bertie encouraged herself, think! What happened to her? And if you don't know, find a way for Viv to avoid answering Rick. She felt rushed...OK, OK. Pulled in one direction and then the other, she finally settled on this, perhaps inadequate background, about how their father had discovered Chris in the throes of withdrawal when he was at his most aggressive and had punched him out before his son could do his own damage. Though Viv had hated seeing them fight, she still loved her brother and when he toppled to the ground, she tried to catch him. He had landed heavily on her and both had rolled down the staircase, crashing against the wall as they went down. Lying in a bundle at the bottom of the stairs, she had noted the huge, bloodied hole in her pants above her left knee. The blade of a knife stuck out from Chris's pocket, colored red from its work on her leg.

"It was an accident," they whispered to Rick. "I don't really want to talk about it."

●●

"Where were you?" Marion stood with her back to the door looking pissed. "I waited for more than an hour at TechTown. I even texted you. Did you forget?"

"Is it already Wednesday?"

"Bertie, I am worried about you."

"Look, we all forget things." She laughed.

"It's not so much your memory that concerns me, but your complete absorption in this new game, this metaverse thing. You spend more time in that world than in ours."

"Oh, you're exaggerating." She gave her a hug. "Stop being so melodramatic. You make things out to be much more than they really are."

"So then, what were you so busy with when I texted? And what were you doing just a few minutes ago when I banged on your door, and you didn't hear it?"

"It's just coincidence that you happened to catch me when I was dealing with something on Venice Beach."

"What about dealing with things right here? Some people need you. For instance, did you give Lisa permission to have Emory hang out at the apartment?"

"Well, yeah, because she wanted someone else to play games with and..."

"Well, she is playing games alright. I walked into the apartment the other day when you were 'busy' and saw Emory with his hand on her leg, just under her skirt."

"No way!" Bertie objected, though her heart missed a beat.

In her head, she swore she would tourniquet Emory's little thing if he ever so much as touched Lisa. To Marion she explained that Emory was just a nerd, probably more interested in touching telescopes than thighs.

"Emory is a terrific kid. Besides, they're only thirteen, for heaven's sake."

"He may well be terrific, but at thirteen even nerds have hormones. Or is he fourteen now?"

She stood in front of Marion feeling like a teenager herself. Part of her wanted to kick back at her. After all, who was she to tell her what to do with her life or how to look after her own grandchild? Neither of Marion's two daughters had kids, so what did she know of grandparenting? Besides, she was just having a little fun. Was that so terrible? Were you not allowed to have your own fun once you became a grandparent? Were you forever after an adjunct to your grandchildren? It seemed to her the women's movement had overlooked a generation, and that people needed reminding that grandmothers were women too. All those popular commercials that once spoke to Bertie of having "come a long way, baby," or which told her to "just do it!"

or encouraged her to indulge herself because she was "worth it," obviously never applied to grandmothers.

"Anyway, Lisa and I spent the morning at TechTown the other day." She made a miserable attempt to justify herself. "We had a great time talking about music."

See, she hadn't dropped the ball. She was still the responsible grandparent encouraging Lisa in her interests and looking after her. Why, her granddaughter was the best thing in her life. What she didn't tell Marion, however, was how impatient she had been when they returned to the apartment. She wanted Lisa to get involved again in her own activities, so she could rush back to Viv who was hanging out in nowhere land, unable to move or speak until Bertie returned and brought her back into existence, into beinghood. After all, Viv needed her breath of life.

She'd been thinking a lot about "being" lately and what it meant to be in this world. She couldn't decide whether she and Viv shared a single "being" when they worked together or were two separate "beings" despite their being conjoined. They merged at the eyes, but Viv was "being" only in Bertie's metaverse when they were one, while she, Bertie, was "being" in Lennie's study separately. So, did that mean that bodily presence had the final say, she wondered, or was it sight that decided what was real? By what metric did one measure it?

Marion watched her with that skewed look on her face as Bertie's mind diverted itself to escape her words.

"C'mon, Bertie, you know I am right. You're fucking up!"

Rick would have had a good time deciphering Bertie's unconscious mind because somewhere in there she recognized she had neglected Lisa, and it devastated her. Just when her granddaughter needed her most, when she was trying to work out her feelings about the coming arrival of a new member of her family, another girl who would be cuter and sweeter than she and might hog her parents' attention and perhaps their affection too, her grandmother had gone AWOL. And now Bertie had made things worse by giving her permission to have a boy in the apartment when her focus lay elsewhere. What was she thinking?

"You're right! You're right!" She started to cry. For heaven's sake, what was wrong with her? If she hadn't been seventy-five, she might have blamed her tearfulness on her periods or menopause, but the only culprit was her and what she had done.

●●

Though Marion didn't mention it when she upbraided her about neglecting Lisa, Bertie knew she also jeopardized her relationship with her and Daru. Not that the three of them didn't have the odd altercation from time to time, but usually they argued about political convictions that turned out to be wrong. One would think that with age, admitting mistakes would be no big deal, but nobody ever said age automatically conferred maturity. On the contrary, being in error made the three of them dig in their heels. They would haul out their phones and make countless checks on Google or DuckDuckGo to prove themselves right. If they only angled their argument in a slightly different way, they imagined, they would find data, somewhere, to confirm what they knew to be correct. If that failed, the claimant might well go off in a sulk!

But disappearing on her friends was a different order of egregious behavior. Friendships were their lifelines. They depended on and needed one another. For all their differences, Marion and Daru were her sisters.

After she married Lennie and moved to Vancouver, his circle of friends had become hers. They were mostly other journalists, but also old high school friends he'd grown up with and who, when they got together, traded in the touchstones of nostalgia. Once she joined Christine at Vancouver General, however, she found her own clique among the nurses and medics there, many of them remaining friends for thirty to forty years. Saying goodbye to them when she and Lennie moved to Seattle to care for Lisa had been the hardest part of relocating. Christine, of course, was dead by then, but there were others whose families were entangled with theirs, their tendrils tightly wound around her heart, drawing her back even as they made their way down the I-5.

Friendships should never be treated lightly. She owed Daru and Marion her full attention and loyalty.

●●

That afternoon, when Lisa arrived after school, Bertie offered to play *Final Fantasy 14* with her. Seeing how thrilled she looked made her feel guilty all over again and she promised herself to make up for her neglect. She began the game where they had left off, with her as the Black Mage, Lisa as Bard, navigating their way to the city of Crystal, Bard singing all the way to fortify her spirits. In her newly acquired yellow Mage hat, Bertie rode her dragon as if she were flying through the pages of Tolkien.

They played alongside each other for a couple of hours, Bertie using her black magic to strengthen Bard's archer's arm so he could protect them. She could feel her attention flagging, however. Constant movement surrounded them, inducing a kind of boredom from the monotony of it all. Bertie tired of avatars perpetually running everywhere, up steps, along roads, across bridges. Couldn't they occasionally walk or just sit still for a moment and enjoy their fantasy surroundings? Why did they never slow down? Touch one another? Hug someone?

After interacting in her own metaverse, the fantasy game made it seem that, if not technologically, at least in terms of maturity, she had slipped back. For one thing, typing her words rather than saying them directly through her avatar resulted in a slight time lapse. "That's because you text so slow," Lisa didn't hesitate to inform her. Still. It meant she had to make her feelings understood by getting her avatar to emote, which it did in standard style, but not in the unique way she could make Viv emote when she moved her own facial and body muscles to match her words.

She didn't want her frustration to get the better of her, but fortunately Lisa decided she had had enough. After the gods of luck awarded her a Nightmare mount, she stood up and stretched.

"Let's have some tea!" she suggested.

Seeing her keen to resume one of their favorite rituals, Bertie was happy to oblige.

When they had settled down at the kitchen table with a cup of Lapsang souchong/Earl Grey, she said, "About Emory coming here in the afternoons..."

"Don't mention that name!"

"I just think we should consider..."

"I don't want to talk about it," she said, cutting her short. "Anyway, Emory won't be coming here again."

Lisa gulped her tea and made a show of adding more sugar to it, though she rarely sweetened her tea. She liked the smoky taste that she said reminded her of volcanoes.

"But I thought you were friends."

"We used to be; we are no longer."

Torn between commiserating with her for having lost a friend and being thankful she had solved the problem of Emory herself, Bertie said nothing more. How sensible she was, her granddaughter. Arielle and Alex had brought her up well and she had her priorities straight. Not so for her grandmother.

# CHAPTER 17

—

AS SOON AS ALEX PICKED UP LISA TO TAKE HER HOME, Bertie ran to her headset. There was still time to be had on Venice Beach; it would not yet be dark. She strapped it on and fastened the new wristlets and vest that Alex said his guys at work wanted her to try again for what he called their haptics. On Venice Beach, most of the crowd were heading home, but outside the beach cottages, the residents had produced bottles of booze and were supposedly toasting the approaching sunset with their friends. From the depths of one cottage, Sonny and Cher harmonized, "I Got You Babe."

The dudes standing around were unlive, but able to perform the specific motion for which they had been programmed, plus make simple conversation. So, they were hanging loose, the unlive ones, their hands holding bottles of beer which they periodically lifted toward their mouths, then down again. Up, down, up, down, gaping clowns at a fair. Jorge was the only live person among them though he wasn't resident there. After watching them for a while, she joined them, exchanging pleas-antries and laughing at Jorge's stupid surf jokes. She even told one of her own that she remembered, about a grandmother whose grandson had been swept out to sea by a gigantic surfing wave. The frantic woman prayed to God to return the boy safe, promising Him that if He answered her prayer, she would never ask for anything else. To her joy, another enormous wave then washed the boy ashore quite unharmed. The grateful woman got down on her knees to thank God, before looking up at the sky and saying, "He had a hat."

Jorge's guffaw delighted her. "Haven't heard that one in a long time," he said in his Russian-accented English.

"You had a Jewish grandmother, didn't you?"

She high-fived Jorge who, responding to their question, forgot about his Latino disguise and regaled them with a story about his *bubbe* who had lived in the family apartment when he was a boy and loved to feed him scary stories about what happened to disobedient boys who refused to eat their supper.

Just then, a light went on without any warning above one of the unmanned surfing dudes, who suddenly sprang alive and ogled them. Who the hell was he, this unexpected newcomer? Alex was supposed to be in control of her metaverse, so what was happening? She wished Alex would alert her when he stuck new avatars in the game. This one, a dreadlocked blonde with ugly scabs on his surfer knees and scars on his elbows, offered her a beer and when she accepted, gave it by placing his arm around her shoulders and bringing the bottle to her mouth. What nerve! Who did he think he was that he could intrude into her space like that? Jake, which turned out to be the new guy's name, watched her drinking, his face right alongside hers. What's his bag? She was missing Rick.

Meanwhile, Jorge had taken one look at this new development and must have decided he didn't like it, for he smacked his bottle against Jake's so hard it flew from his hand and smashed to the ground. Beer sprayed everywhere and she should have been moving her hand to her cheek to wipe off the splashes and check that neither she nor Viv were hurt, but something else happened contiguous with the smash that so threw her that for a moment Bertie didn't know who she was or where. When the bottle against Viv's cheek juddered against the one thrown by Jorge, Bertie felt the vibration in her own cheek. If not quite instantaneous—maybe a lag of a second or two—it nevertheless happened, she was sure of it. Her palm pressed against her cheek could still feel the aftereffect, a tiny quivering pulse. And then it was over.

By the time her attention returned to the scene, Jorge had split. She saw him dragging a struggling Jake down the beach. He had him in a chokehold, which seemed a bit overkill. When the lights above Jake's head went out, Jorge ditched him like an empty sack and walked off into the distance.

Enter Rick, rushed and flushed, as if he had just woken from a deep sleep. No Rip Van Winkle though, he immediately made a beeline for her and Viv.

"Are you OK?" he asked, touching their cheek, and looking as if he were really concerned.

Impressive, Bertie thought, as his hand glided gently over her skin, looking for abrasions or cuts, she assumed. Then, an amazing thing happened. He turned his head away from Viv, and Bertie swore she heard him whisper something that sounded like "Doggle." Surely that word was intended for her, not Viv. After all, "Doggle," the gaming company, would have meant nothing to Viv. It must have been a message that Rick-bro intended for Bertie, to alert her. Now, she wondered if, in that momentary lapse in her attention when she experienced the trembling, she had unwittingly allowed a Doggle intruder to steal Alex's secrets. She hit her forehead with the heel of her hand. Barely a month into her reign as master of her Venice Beach metaverse, she had already endangered Alex and his team's findings. It was all her fault.

Even if that were true, she had no idea what to do about it. Jorge seemed to have destroyed the spy's avatar, so maybe he would contact Alex to report the intrusion. Surely, Alex could then alter his algorithms and close whatever portal had tempted the Doggle spy in the first place. Doggle, of course, was not the only company that had spies out there. Every big technological concern tested the waters for ways into their competitors' sites.

Too much was happening. Rick led her away from the fantasy drinking squad and they walked together along the sand until he found a little hillock with a few stray strands of grass stuck in it. With their backs against the hillock and their legs drawn up, they had a comfortable viewing position of the theater that in thirty minutes would present the Californian sunset. Pulling a light blanket from his bag because the nights at Venice Beach could become cool, Rick threw it over her legs and put his arm around her shoulders. Instinctively, she dropped her head into the crux of his shoulder, her cheek pressed against his chest, giving her a direct view of his lower body. Even if she said so herself, Bertie had become pretty quick at maneuvering Viv, though perhaps not quite as accurate as Rick-bro who lifted Rick's hand and gently stroked Viv's hair and pulled some strands behind her ear. Man, he was good.

That's when Bertie realized she had not given Viv a sexual history, so she was playing blindly with her reactions to sexual overtures. Up to this point, she had depicted her as slightly innocent in her interactions with men, receptive rather than proactive, yet as a woman of twenty-seven, she must have had some history. The way she had held her own in the beginning when a suspicious Jorge had tried to stop her from speaking to

Rick certainly suggested she was no pushover and had experience with male attention. Given her history as Bertie had plotted it, she decided she had lost her virginity at sixteen while still in Merced High School. A Latino classmate, Mario, had pledged his everlasting love and she had fallen for him, despite her father's racist objections. Believing she had found the love of her life, Viv tried to keep her private life from her parents, like her brother had. She imagined how she and Mario would marry once they graduated and make a home in Merced, but Uncle Sam had different plans for the young man. A low number in the draft lottery of '69 had sent him to training camp and ultimately to Vietnam, from which he never returned. Viv never forgot her first love, but whereas the loss of Chris had sworn her off drugs entirely, the death of Mario drove her to seek him in other Latinos. For the next couple of years, she dated only Latinos.

As for her sexual activities, Bertie assumed once Viv moved to the LA area, and had a few other relationships under her belt, she was comfortable with her sexuality. It felt strange imagining what Viv would be like in bed with Jorge or Rick when all she had to go by was her own experience. Though women shared reports with other women about their dates, they seldom spoke about what they had felt. It also didn't seem fair to impose her own experience on Viv, especially since her responses were to someone who hemorrhaged words in the build-up to lovemaking, but in the act scattered words as if he had no idea of syntax. His endearments came strewn, uneven, and broken up with small dashes and ellipses. She loved it. But what would Viv love?

"Viv!" Someone called her.

"Yes," Bertie responded immediately, turning around to see Daru and Marion standing at the door to Lennie's study, looking at her as if she were a lab rat in an experiment.

"See!" Marion pointed at her. "I told you she could no longer tell."

Daru nodded sadly, then the two of them closed the door and left, leaving her gazing after them, and wondering what it was all about. What did they want? They had interrupted her at an important junction in Viv's relationship with Rick, and she needed to get back to Rick's arms.

While she still lay on the warm sand, the sun crept closer to the horizon until it looked like a distorted Humpty Dumpty about to fall off the world. The streaks of color that had accompanied its descent still radiated red, orange, and yellow wavelengths.

"Watch for the green streak," Rick encouraged her, but at the same time he worked his toes under her foot and rubbed against her arch under the blanket.

Bertie's own arch curled as if it had been tickled. Viv immediately pulled up her leg, then laughingly admitted to having ticklish feet.

"What about ticklish legs?"

This time his hand must have slipped up her inner thigh for again Bertie felt it on her own body. Her leg recoiled in shock, which was not what she'd meant Viv to do. What the...? She didn't know what was happening. She couldn't say it felt terrible. In fact, the sensation was rather pleasant, which is what disturbed her. It felt good. In the meantime, Rick was nothing but persistent and his fingers soon started inching up, crawling to within an inch of Viv's underpants. Bertie's own thigh...

She panicked. She bashed the off switch, and the fingers disappeared along with the two avatars.

When she removed her headset, she checked her thigh, although she had no idea what she expected to see. Certainly nothing appeared different, just the same old flabby lady thigh.

Yet she was sure she had experienced something impossible, as if the real world and her digital one had touched and opened a passageway between them. She sat back in Lennie's chair staring into space. She tried to understand what seemed beyond the laws of physics. After all, this wasn't a movie with special effects.

Then a more disturbing thought occurred to Bertie that completely displaced her earlier thoughts about space-time. If she had experienced the sensation that Rick had been trying to stimulate in Viv, would Rick-bro feel something too if Viv were to touch his avatar? If she pressed her body against Rick's and he pressed back, would both Rick-bro and she feel their intimacy together? She sat up in the chair, feeling shocked. This was ridiculous! No, no, no. She was horrified. It was bad enough being a voyeur, but mediated sex? Uh-uh, she shook her head. Not possible. She must have been imagining it. She had probably been so engrossed in what was happening she thought she felt something. Maybe she was just being protective of Viv, like Geppetto when the fox led Pinocchio astray in the Land of Boobies.

# CHAPTER 18

SHE HAD DECIDED IT WAS TIME TO TAKE A BREAK, CATCH her breath for a few days. Her brush with the Doggle spy had left her heart racing and her sleep upended. Fearing she had unwittingly dropped the ball and allowed a spy to infiltrate Sarssein and jeopardize her son-in-law's business, she cautiously sounded him out at dinner on Friday night. To her surprise, Alex laughed at her fears and shook his head, relieving her of further doses of guilt. It was his custom, he told her, to release false spies into each of his projects as a way of checking that his employees remained alert. His staff never knew when to expect one nor if a suspected spy would turn out to be one of theirs or a real infiltrator from one of their competitors. It kept them on their toes, he said.

Bertie's relief at his words proved temporary, however, for that night, lying in bed listening to the air-conditioning unit's heavy breathing, she realized she was an employee of Sarssein. Although her 3D world had been a birthday present, perhaps "loan" was the more appropriate term. Even "office" or "lab" seemed more accurate. And she had thought of herself as "the man," she laughed, "the boss" of her little world. No matter which way she saw it, Sarssein held the reins and at any time Alex could send a spy into her realm to check not only on Jorge, but on her too.

The spy incident, however, was not the only one pushing her to take a break and reassess where she stood. She needed time to absorb what she had just experienced with Rick-bro in the metaverse and examine it outside of its sexual context. Not that she had any desire to stop Viv from having sex, or rather pretend sex, with Rick. After all, she was the controller, a limited one as she now saw it, who had placed her in situations that might arguably lead to intimacy. Besides, seeing Viv having fun and romance fulfilled her own nostalgia for the good old days which, until Marion described it as living vicariously, she'd thought would be an interesting, perhaps even enlightening, experience. Who didn't want to reexamine various periods of her life? And if an avatar helped do it, why not? As one gets closer to the celestial end zone, shaping your life story sometimes takes precedence over more concrete things.

Perhaps that was why she made Viv and Rick's mediated sex play so unsophisticated—in a lot of ways, so innocent. She certainly had read plenty of erotic novels and seen enough disturbing Netflix movies to be aware of the nastiness of sex today. Since pornography had inserted itself sinuously into everyday lives, its sordid, grungy nature had become common knowledge. Any high school kid who could switch on a computer knew who did what to whom and into which orifice. She had no doubt that even Lisa had familiarity with the vocabulary of sex. Back in the sixties and seventies, she swore things were different. Ignorance and innocence abounded, and women desired to be wooed slowly. They wanted to flirt and follow the game romantically from its first-base moves to its crescendo end. Sometimes when she listened to the rock music lyrics from that time and compared them to the cruel and degrading words of today's songs, they seemed positively innocent. That's the way it was with sex too. Despite today's hullabaloo about boomers' free love attitudes, sex actually had a childlike playfulness about it then. Even when it was free, it was never ugly.

Good God! She was starting to sound like an old fart who sees the past through the wrong end of a rose-tinted telescope, Bertie thought. Maybe she really was getting old, edging her memories with nostalgic gilt for something that maybe had not even existed.

●●

"Do you think I live too much in the past?" she asked Arielle who sat on the opposite side of the table at Jae's, the Japanese restaurant close to Children's Hospital. They were having one of their mother/daughter lunches, a special alone time together that she relished. Even so, their lunches rarely stretched beyond an hour because Arielle had to return to duty by two. Given the rush, Bertie often came armed with questions.

"Probably," she answered, with a *nigiri* shrimp and avocado roll in her mouth. Her daughter never minced her words. "But at your age, it's natural you would spend time in the past. You are trying to control it. That's why you always bring old photos into the present. You want to remind me what I was like as a child and you still ran my life."

"As if I could ever have run your life! You took charge of yourself right from the start."

At an early age, Arielle had decided the exact trajectory of her life and had propelled herself in that direction with the persistence of a torpedo heading for its target. She would become a doctor, she promised when she was still only eight. In preparation for her future, she set up her dolls in her makeshift hospital and treated them one by one for cuts and abrasions, broken legs, and runny tummies. To Bertie's concern at the time, she would often wound her patients purposely so she could console and heal them. She had a bright-red pen with which she drew slashes and grisly lacerations on their plastic bodies, plus a blue pen to indicate bruises and shadows beneath the eyes. Occasionally, she even bit off a doll's finger or broke an arm, so she could practice stanching blood flow and knotting arm slings. Bertie worried about her.

Yet today, her patients adored her, often praising her calm and competency, but more often her empathy. She could feel the existential fear they camouflaged in their formal questions about doses and side effects.

Arielle had been a quiet child and bookish like her father. So, her daily after-school cutthroat interactions with her dolls surprised Bertie, who had tried to introduce her to her own interests, which tended toward physical exercise. But nothing about swimming, kayaking, or running ever caught her daughter's attention like medicine. In retrospect, Bertie had probably brought her work home too often, exposing the child to a blood-and-guts world that sounded more real to her than that of *The Lion, the Witch and the Wardrobe*. No one she knew would ever think of walking through the back of a wardrobe, she had told her mother when still a second grader. As hungry a reader as she was, she had never been one for fantasy but leaned instead toward real-life stories in which brave characters moved mountains to save their families or to prevent a world catastrophe. As far as Arielle was concerned, only heroes and saviors filled her mother's bloody domain. In fact, the nurses and doctors felt anything but heroic. Wearied to the bone, they simply carried on like automatons. They had no choice. Where there was need, they did their duty.

"You look wonderful," she said as she patted her daughter's arm.

Pregnancy suited Arielle. Despite how hard she worked and how tired she often felt, her intense teal eyes shone clear and bright, her fair hair glossy like the old Breck shampoo ads Bertie remembered from her girlhood days. At seven and a half months, Arielle carried a small tight belly that sat high and made her look younger than her forty-five years. Occasionally, a fist or a knee would shift inside her and she would grab Bertie's hand and hold it to her stomach so she could feel her new grandchild and share the joy. How lucky Bertie felt to have a second granddaughter on the way.

Despite her joy, however, she couldn't help wondering whether her experiencing her daughter's feeling was yet another mediated encounter, as in the metaverse. Was it also vicarious?

Stop it! she told herself. Sometimes a cigar is just a cigar.

The rest of their conversation revolved around practicalities, like buying new baby gear, and baby clothes. Gone were the pram and cot from Lisa's early days, even the tiny sweaters she had knitted her in bright colors to defy the gender conformists who still insisted on pink and blue. For the new baby, Bertie decided she would knit a blanket in the softest wool she could find.

"I can still remember how I felt carrying Lisa thirteen years ago." Arielle smiled, laying down her chopsticks. "It was all so strange. I thought my hospital work with babies had made me an expert and I would take pregnancy in stride. How wrong I was! The whole experience made me a nervous wreck. Who would have thought? I was much more scared than a pregnant 16-year-old who knew nothing about what could go wrong inside there."

Even as she said the words, Arielle patted her belly reassuringly.

"You certainly never let on that you were scared, not even to me."

"Especially not to you," she laughed, folding her napkin, and standing up.

"Is it time? Do you have to get back already?"

"Bye, Mom." She kissed Bertie on the cheek. "Oh. By the way, Alex says to tell you the guy in his lab working in your metaverse told him it was amazing how quickly you got the hang of things. The way you handle your avatar is—I quote him—pretty impressive."

Bertie glowed at the compliment and had to stop herself from asking Arielle whether he had said anything else. After her daughter left, she drank her green tea and wondered how she could find out more about Rick-bro, even though in the back of her head, she could still hear Marion haranguing her about her absorption in this other world.

"Game, schmame!" Marion had attempted to bring her back when she'd put the metaverse on the same ludic plane as *Final Fantasy*. "Look, I only want to protect you from getting in too deep. I've been reading up about this stuff since you got so involved and it's much too powerful for a game. And, even if it were just a game," she added casually, digging in her big black bag for her lip gloss as if what she was about to say represented an afterthought when she must have been wanting to lecture Bertie all along, "you are treating it as if it were real, Bertie. Viv's not real. She's not alive. She's not a being. She cannot think nor reflect."

In the silence that followed, she grappled with Marion's words that on the surface appeared obvious and rational. Of course, she knew Viv wasn't real, and she wasn't alive. Yet hadn't she given Viv life? Contingent life, yes, but nevertheless a kind of "being there" that enabled her to live in the sun on Venice Beach and have a relationship with Rick. Without Bertie, her avatar did not exist at all. Whereas when Bertie awakened her, gave her the breath of life with her words and actions, the two of them constituted one. They were conjoined beings, symbiotic, even. If she could only find the right words to match what she felt inside, she could make Marion understand. But the more she thought about her relationship with Viv, the greater the entanglement became in her mind. Even as she reached for understanding, her thoughts escaped like slippery fish before she could haul them in, leaving her standing flat-footed in a boat to nowhere, wondering if when she played in the metaverse and gave her own being to Viv, she, Bertie, disappeared. *She* wasn't there, *she* wasn't "being." Can you "be" when your "being" is mediated through a nonbeing?

Feeling defensive and wanting to escape her own circular thoughts, she had challenged Marion.

"So, you tell me, then. What does it mean to be real? Maybe we are all living in a simulation, and we don't even know it."

Marion sighed, as if wondering how to escape from this existential quagmire of a conversation, but who was she to say they weren't simply avatars in someone else's metaverse. Maybe God Himself lived vicariously through their lives, getting His kicks every time one of His avatars fell on her arse.

"You call this real?" Bertie pointed to the empty apartment around her. "Living on my own, doing the same things day in and day out, ignored by the rest of the world? How real a life is that?"

"As real as mine."

Marion had cupped her chin and looked her in the eye. She saw the vulnerability she knew her friend carried deep inside.

Her smile spoke of hurt, of bruising. Though Marion seldom mentioned her ex except to disparage him, once when they were chatting at TechTown, she confessed, throwing her pride to the wind, she had begged Jeremy to stay, not to abandon her and the girls. But, days later when Bertie referred to something she had said, she denied even remembering the conversation when she had sobbed and let it all flow out painfully unexpurgated. About her two daughters who had chosen ten years ago to live far away from their mother, she remained mum too, though Bertie knew how much their decision hurt her friend. Though Marion flew to London once a year to visit Megan and Laura, she pined for the kind of closeness she once imagined they would share. Their difficult teenage years spent during her period of single parenthood after her divorce from Jeremy remained uppermost in their minds and neither girl remembered the years of their childhood when their mother had given them her best. Only Marion's stress, exhaustion, and impatience, while trying to hold things together as a New York litigator, cook, and spurned wife, did they recall. What kind of flaw in human design allowed memory to come into play only at age four, Bertie wondered, when parents endowed so much love, effort, and suffering into those first four years.

The waiter brought her the check, and she returned to her world in South Lake Union. She parked her car in the underground garage and changed elevators on the main floor, greeting the new concierge who, unlike Michael, made no move to offer help of any sort. Not that her doggy bag weighed much more than a few ounces, but still, she missed Michael. The new guy was certainly pleasant enough and talkative. After a few conversations, she'd discovered he had been stringing his girlfriend along for at least two years.

"Has she dumped you yet?" she asked.

"Nah, Mrs. Glazer. She loves me too much," he replied, smiling impishly.

As the pelvic elevator door opened, Daru stepped out dressed in a new professional-looking jacket similar to the kind she used to wear on her news broadcasts a decade earlier. Now, however, a soft pleated skirt replaced the tight pencil one that had defined her image then. Her face too had softened since those days. On her feet, she wore the shoes they had bought together at Lindstrom.

"Hi, there. Where are you off to looking so splendid?"

Daru's eyes showed the same sparkle and intelligence they had worn during her nightly broadcasts. She was alert, alive, and on the ball. Gone was the sadness that had crippled her after Aditya's death and left her labile.

"I'm off to teach my new class!" She grinned, bouncing on her feet, raring to go.

Bertie had no idea what she was talking about, so it took her a while to put the pieces together without showing her ignorance. Had Daru told her before about the ageism classes she planned to teach in city high schools, and she had simply forgotten? Or been too engrossed in Viv and Rick?

"What got me started," Daru informed her, "was this Yale professor I read about, who earlier this year advocated hara-kiri for old codgers in Japan." At Bertie's recoil, she confirmed, that yes, hara-kiri was what he said; she hadn't misread him. "Too many aged people in the population defeated the economy, so he urged the old to do the right thing and disembowel themselves for their community. Make the ultimate sacrifice, he'd written, and correct the country's demographics."

In the chilled silence that followed her words, Bertie stared at her friend in disbelief, but Daru had already moved ahead, spurred on by her newfound enthusiasm for reaching the kids before they acquired this less acknowledged American bias. With them, she approached the problem by breaking down ageism into specific acts—like rushing the old man who takes too long at the cashier, or not bothering to greet the old woman who said hello, or pushing past a group of the elderly chatting on the sidewalk. "And the kids get it straight away. They don't mean any harm. It's just that you don't matter to them as much as their peers do."

Of course, it helped Daru's cause with the kids that she had once been a TV newscaster and so, by some process of celebrity shading, they didn't place her in the same category as "old people." Yes, she was old, as far as they were concerned, but she trailed glamorous images of TV lights and cameras. Certainly, she was younger than Bertie and Marion, "old people" that they were, not that Bertie would ever argue over a few years. Still, the period between one's sixties and seventies seemed to her a critical one, the beginning of the accelerated downslide. One's sixties might have been the new fifties, but nobody quoted the seventies as the new sixties, not even in the fashion magazines. There, they just stayed quiet as if women of that age lived beyond the pale.

Bertie felt full of admiration for Daru. "You're getting them at the right age and educating a whole generation about empathy."

"Or even just politeness. Simple politeness keeps the social fabric from unraveling. Without it..."

"Without it, we have the kind of chaos we see in politics today."

On that note, Daru moved off and Bertie returned to apartment 2045 wondering what she could do to contribute to the betterment of life. Her nursing role had satisfied her at the time, but that service was long over, and she had done nothing important since then other than the work she assumed for the party, rustling up voters, phoning her representatives, or demonstrating her support for women and their interests, which of course were humankind's interests. She still felt a huge, gaping hole in this last quarter of her life. She wanted to matter in the big scheme of things, but she didn't know how. She tried to convince herself the experimenting she had undertaken for Alex could turn out to be part of the new existential revolution the metaverse prophesied, but somehow, she couldn't divorce that theorctical idea from its other more visceral part which had sent her running for cover just yesterday.

When she opened her door, she was surprised to find Lisa already there. The apartment smelled like toasted bagels and on the table sat two empty plates speckled with crumbs. Bertie looked around, but there was nobody else there. Next to the plates lay a selfie that showed Lisa and Emory kissing "ironically." At least that's how she read it given the kids' raised eyebrows and melodramatic expressions. Lisa never took selfies and often made fun of girls who walked around snapping pictures of themselves, like trees falling in the forest, fearing nobody would hear them if they weren't recorded. She squelched a simmering sense of disquiet. They were just kids.

"Wanna play?" Lisa had the computer open at *Overwatch 2.* Metal monsters already teleported around the screen looking fierce as they threatened all with their axes, javelins, grenades, and mines.

"But I want to be Mei, OK?"

Mei was the damage hero who could shoot projectiles that encased her enemies in ice preventing them from moving. She also surrounded herself in blocks of ice to become invulnerable.

"Who should I be then?"

"You can be my ally, Zarya."

"So, remind me, what does Zarya do?"

"She's like a grandma. She absorbs all incoming damage. Ready?"

# CHAPTER 19

---

"GRAN, ARE YOU STILL IN YOUR PAJAMAS?"

"What? Oh, these? You mean my new-fashion pajama look?" She twirled around like a Victoria's Secret model. "What do you think? I see lots of people your age wearing pajama bottoms with their sweaters."

Lisa offered up a tiny, indulgent smile, but Bertie knew she already tired of her grandmother's behavior. So, she offered her another reason for her slovenly appearance, suggesting she had a sore stomach and planned to jump into bed early. She rubbed the offending area and smoothed her unbrushed hair that had been made worse by four hours under the tight-fitting headset.

"You and the aunties always have stomach complaints. If it's not constipation, it's diarrhea! Will I be like that too when I'm your age?"

"If that's the only complaint you have when you're my age"— she tousled Lisa's hair—"you will be one lucky woman."

She groaned. "And what about arthritis?"

"Yeah, I'm afraid that's another one. Daru has it badly in her left leg."

"By the way," she said, as she unpacked her homework, "Daru asked if you were still stuck in the metaverse because she and Marion haven't seen you in days and only know you're not dead because I told them so."

"What are they fussing about?" Bertie said, annoyed they had spoken of death to her granddaughter. "I've been here all the time. All they need do is knock on the door." She caught a skeptical look cross Lisa's face before she turned away and busied herself with some school papers. A headline on one of them asked: "Does the US have an empire?" a topic most likely not seen in many American schools. She would have loved to help Lisa with that one, but just couldn't pull herself together enough to organize her thoughts. Instead she told her she would lie down in Lennie's study for a while until her ache went away. "In the meantime," she encouraged her, "grab yourself something to eat."

Still in her big boots, Lisa galumphed into the kitchen, and Bertie heard her banging one cupboard after another, followed by rummaging in the fridge.

"There's absolutely nothing to eat in here, Gran. No more bagels, no juice..."

●●

He stood on her doorstep chewing at the nail on the baby finger of his right hand. Looking at him through the peephole in her door, his head looked enormous to Bertie, his feet in their Doc Martens miles away. Could she pretend she wasn't there and just stay quiet until he went away? She peeped at him again, but this time, he put his own eye to the glass, looking straight at her. She hurriedly pulled back the latch.

"Hi, Mrs. Glazer."

"Hello, there, Emory. What brings you here on a Saturday morning?" She poked her disheveled head out the door, hiding the rest of her body, though she saw the boy's eyes quickly take in the rumpled, striped pajamas, and the splotch of hardened muesli by the neckline. She politely invited him in, but to her relief, he had no wish to stay.

"It's just that...I mean..." He looked at his feet and swallowed. In all the time she had known Lisa's young friend, he had never been tongue-tied. If anything, Emory never stopped talking, as if the thoughts that flashed through his constantly engaged brain just rolled out in a continuous stream. Now, he stuttered and scratched the side of his neck.

"Can I ask you something?"

"Of course, Emory."

"Do you know what gives with Lisa? She's acting weird."

"Weird, how?" she asked, twisting her hair behind her ears in a vague effort to look...what?...tidy, she supposed, less like a homeless woman, a woman caught between two homes. Emory with his interest in multiverses might even have understood that only one of her stood before him. Another frolicked in the sun on Venice Beach with a tall blonde man named Rick.

"Ever since this Jared guy started bugging her, she's been... Well, he keeps phoning her, even though she's told him to leave her alone."

What a glutton for punishment, Bertie thought.

"And now, he must have finally worn her down because I think she's hanging out with him."

She didn't like the sound of that, but maybe Jared and Lisa had come to some sort of reconciliation. It wasn't her job to police her friends.

"Also..." he began. Then, as if thinking better of it, looked away, avoiding her eyes. He nibbled again on the nail of his pinkie.

Of course, his hesitation immediately got her attention, and she pressed him, only to find out that Lisa and Jared had been spray-painting graffiti just a block from their school, splattering thick curlicues of black paint on any white surface they could find.

"'It all sucks,' the words read. And Lisa's tag was 'Viv.'"

"Viv! Viv?"

Alarm bells should have gone off, but she was incapable of hearing them. Instead, other contradictory thoughts swirled round her head. Lisa was a free agent, capable of making her own friends. No, she's still a kid. What the hell does she think she's doing? But all kids get into mischief. She will land herself in trouble. Should Bertie warn her? Should she tell her mother? In her distracted state, she couldn't translate any of these thoughts into a plan of action.

Before Bertie could dwell on it any further, however, Emory confessed to yet another problem, one perhaps of more immediate concern to him. Without telling him, Lisa had given up on their comic strip, which meant they couldn't complete it in time to enter the Great Cosmic Comic Competition, which he was certain they could win. Only she knew how their otherworldly story would end.

"Did you perhaps do something to annoy her, Emory?" she asked, remembering what Marion had said about seeing the boy's hand on Lisa's leg.

"Not that I know of, Mrs. Glazer. Lisa's never been one to hold back if something annoys her. Like she's said plenty about the baby and how she feels about it, how it will intrude on her life, and all that. But if you ask me, I think she can't wait to have a sister to fuss over. About anything else though, she hasn't said a word. Nothing, as far as I can remember. Except..."

Eschewing his nail biting, he held his chin in his hand and screwed up his lips sideways like Roman in the TV series

*Succession*, looking sophisticatedly amused when in fact there wasn't a contrived bone in the boy's body. Emory was nothing but sincere. She knew him.

"You remember something?"

"Well, the other day, like, just out of the blue, Lisa said our comic strip stank. It was too childish for her. 'Puerile' was the word she used."

●●

Bertie's break from Viv, Rick, and Rick-bro lasted four days. After the second day, she felt she had forgotten something, like leaving part of herself on Venice Beach. It still stood there alone wondering where she had gone. Curiosity got the better of her and, by the fourth day, pushing aside any concerns about Lisa, she returned to Ocean Front Walk where she paraded Viv in all her seventies glamor. Daru had been right that an eye-catching appearance would prove a door-opener and make connections happen quickly. Rick-bro had taken the lead and Bertie found herself responding through Viv rather than setting the agenda. Rick had invited her to lunch at one of the Mexican restaurants just up the road from the beach, but still within her VR radius and soon the two of them sat ensconced at an open-air table by a window. The new "Waterloo" hit from Abba, that had won the 1974 Eurovision Song Contest in Brighton, could be heard everywhere, including at Restaurante Mi Casita. Viv now wore her hair in a ponytail, along with the new headphones Bertie had bought hanging around her neck. When Rick excused himself to go to the bathroom, she plugged them in for a quick listen to the Beach Boys singing "Help Me, Rhonda."

Meanwhile, Bertie sweated beneath the wristlets and vest that Alex's staff had given her to wear. Without knowing their purpose, she didn't see the point of keeping them on. With Viv about to eat a meal requiring a knife and fork, she needed all her wits about her. Even if she ate, or rather pretend-ate, rice with a spoon, Bertie still had to ensure the grains didn't fall all over her. Viv needed to balance the spoon or fork near her mouth for at least a couple of seconds. It would not be easy.

Just before she ripped off the bands and laid them on Lennie's desk, Rick returned to Viv's table. In 1974, he would have smelt of patchouli. It was easy to imagine that Rick might have sprayed himself with it, for most Venice Beach restaurants at the time stocked their bathrooms with the scent. Between patchouli and dope, one couldn't go anywhere in the neighborhood before being assaulted with their reek which sooner or later permeated one's clothes. But how they had loved it then. It made them feel they belonged to the same blissful community. Anyone who smelled of something else, eau de cologne, for instance, must surely have been an outsider. It was all very superficial, but that is how it was then, at least for the length of Bertie's stay. She would return to her blood-and-guts job within the week.

Over the last few days, Rick and Viv had become comfortable with each other and strolled hand in hand most of the time. It took some doing on Bertie's part to link their fingers, but eventually she managed to get it right. Rick-bro seemed to have it down pat from the beginning despite his proxy sporting a big metal ring on one finger. Surely Rick-bro had been playing with avatars for some time before turning up on Venice Beach. Anyway, he was certainly upping the ante in the affection arena. Once, in a brief check of her side mirror, she saw him stroking Viv's hair while he talked. Most likely an absent-minded gesture, but nevertheless one that expressed intimacy, perhaps even tenderness. So, when she noticed he was playing footsie with Viv under the table too, she wasn't at all surprised.

What bothered her was this time, she, herself, felt nothing. When their bare feet rubbed together, no corresponding sensation flickered in her feet, not even a tickle. Nor had she felt anything earlier when they clasped hands or when he stroked her hair. She couldn't understand it. She swore the last time they touched it had caused reverberations in her body, like… like…She had a hard time naming the flutterings, though she knew very well what they were, just like pedicurists know when they push certain pressure points under one's feet. Even though the young women with their powerful fingers look away nonchalantly, they are well aware of how good they make their customers feel.

As if that shift of vicarious feeling from present to absent wasn't enough, Bertie had also noticed subtle changes in Viv's conversation. She had gained many new, sophisticated words and phrases in response to the broader scope of Rick's conversation over the last few days. That too confused Bertie. Given how frivolous she had purposely made the whole scene between them, when Rick talked politics to her, she wondered if perhaps another handler had taken over from Rick-bro. Yet the voice remained the same; it was still Rick-bro, whoever he was. With an odd sentence here and another comment there, he had subtly redirected the conversation to topics of more substance, until their talk circled to global affairs, like the troubles in Ireland, the earthquake in China, and the Carnation Revolution in Portugal. Soon, they were arguing, each giving his and her personal take on the subject.

How could she resist?

Soon, she was knee-deep with Rick-bro, expounding with feeling why she thought Rick had missed the point; Rick-bro coming back with equally forceful comments through his avatar. For a moment, she felt as if she were sparring with Lennie, each of them playfully jabbing where they thought it would most disturb. Without her noticing, Viv and Rick's relationship had deepened and become more complex, perhaps more evenly matched, not unlike her own and Lennie's. And When Rick in a jocular aside said, "The phoenix rises again from the ashes," which had always been one of Lennie's tactics when she thought he was down and out, only to see him bounce back with a new and intricate angle, the whole scene before her eyes unnerved her.

She sat down, feeling suddenly off-balance. She knew it was all illogical and unreal to hear Lennie, but then, given her ignorance about metaverse algorithms, she could believe anything. For all she knew, someone had discovered a way to connect the deceased with survivors at home so they could provide company and solace.

"Viv?" Rick sounded concerned when Viv remained silent. He asked, "What are you thinking about?"

If Bertie listened hard enough, his voice sounded just a little like Lennie's, especially when he cajoled Viv, taking her chin in his hand and pulling it toward him as if to touch lips. And when he laughed at her retort, she could swear the sound had the same staccato cutoff at the end as Lennie's. It so spooked Bertie that she hurriedly switched off the scene and sat stewing in her own confusion while regaining her sense of reality. If it wasn't Lennie, could someone be playing with her head? Could Lisa be inserting herself into Bertie's magical world and assuming Lennie's persona? If Lisa thought her grandmother flirted with Rick-bro, maybe her sense of loyalty to her grandfather could drive her to run interference on his behalf. Bertie was sinking to a new low, doubting her granddaughter, but she couldn't help her suspicions which, like fast-growing ivy moving up a trellis, planted their suckers in her thoughts. If Lisa could borrow Alex's headset without his knowing, why would she stop at accessing his computer?

In her hand, the two controllers felt heavy with consequence. If she pressed the grip…if she didn't press it…

But hadn't Lisa already told her she had little interest in Bertie's metaverse? It was her own she yearned for. Besides, this year promised her more excitement than the seventies, which was half a century ago, for heaven's sake.

"Pu-u-leeze!" she'd retorted that earlier time when Bertie had checked whether she'd entered her space. "It's much too boring for me."

Bertie ripped out the ivy's suckers and freed herself of her disloyal thoughts about Lisa. Fearing for her own mind, she lay down the headset and controllers, and to reorient herself, stood momentarily at the window staring out at the familiar ocean. Yes, Leonard was gone, dead, his ashes strewn by her on that same piece of ocean, the Puget Sound, his atoms absorbed by whales, salmon, and mussels, themselves perhaps incorporated into yet other life-forms struggling for survival in the water's depths. Nothing of him remained that hadn't suffered a sea change.

She replaced the headset, took a deep breath, and pressed the button. And there they still were, Viv and Rick, gazing at each other across the table, their bodies leaning forward, as if they needed to touch faces, hands, and shoulders. Looking at them, anyone could recognize the intimacy they shared, or for that matter, the closeness their controllers shared. Yet what she felt most was befuddled. If Rick-bro wasn't Lennie or Lisa, then who the hell was he, this avatar-handler who sounded like Lennie? What if he didn't appreciate smart-talking, political women? Caught up in her enthusiasm for conversation, had she unwittingly turned Viv into a mini-me without knowing how Rick-bro would respond?

In a retro move, she touched Rick's knee and smiled, but it wasn't necessary, for nothing she said drove him away. If anything, the more they brought to their discussions, the greater his affection. Suddenly, he stood up, and for a moment Bertie thought he might walk out on her, but no. He came to her side of the table, lifted her from her chair so she stood next to him, and then gave her one of the most passionate kisses Bertie had experienced in a long time.

●●

"The guys at work have been asking if you have any feedback on the neural armbands or vest?" Alex asked Bertie at their dinner on Friday night.

Arielle had picked up a low-spice Thai meal from the local restaurant which, since Covid, had removed all its tables and transformed itself into a take-out place. "Low-spice" still had a kick to it and Bertie wondered if this baby girl would arrive in the world with a penchant for hot, spicy food. At the Levians' home, their glass dining room table already displayed splatters of Thai sauce and grains of rice.

"Rather uncomfortable, and the vest felt like Spanx, or some kind of girdle. It was so tight. They made me sweat, so I took them off."

"Darn! So, you didn't actually experience the haptic effect?"

"The what effect?"

"The haptic effect or tactile effect. It's something that allows you to feel any physical pressure your avatar feels. So, for example, if Vivienne strikes a rock with a sword—though she's probably not playing with swords on Venice Beach"—he laughed at his own joke—"you might feel a tiny vibration in your arm when her sword makes contact."

"That's what the armbands do?"

"They're supposed to, but since you don't seem to have experienced it, maybe I'll ask the guys to increase the effect of the connection."

She decided not to argue, though she had indeed experienced something strange earlier. She just didn't know exactly what it was, or who was making her feel it. Was it simply the algorithm or did the person who controlled Rick make the calls? Squeezing anything out of Alex without sounding like she had some agenda, however, proved impossible.

"One of the lab guys will know how to get just enough connectivity to make you feel involved, without knocking you over the head with Viv's movements. Balance is what we're looking for," he offered, patting his wife's tummy which had expanded in the last few weeks so that she was now obliged to wear loose smock-type blouses to the hospital.

In her eighth month, her daughter looked radiant. Her hair shone; her cheeks glowed.

But what age is he and what does he look like? Bertie wondered. Neither were simple questions to ask of your son-in-law who would most likely have shrugged. Only Rick-bro's technological expertise interested Alex.

# CHAPTER 20

———

AS SOON AS SHE GOT HOME, BERTIE SWITCHED ON THE VR headset and snapped the neural bands snuggly between wrist and elbow. The vest still felt uncomfortable, but she bore it like a stoic Victorian heroine. It was 10:00 p.m. and Venice Beach looked mostly deserted, but she felt ready. The usual drinking parties still spilled from the bungalows onto the path, but most of the drifting crowd had gone. From time to time, a drug dealer would stop by one of the bungalows to offer LSD, angel dust, and speed, but he soon wandered off, muttering about the area's oversaturation. On the beach, a spaced-out group lay around a bonfire, though making fires on the beach was illegal even then. In their midst, a young man with flowing hair that fell forward over his guitar strummed "Starry, Starry Night" and sang quietly in the pitch dark of "flaming flowers" and of colors that changed hues.

Who were these live people? It was as if the toys—Alex's NPCs—had come to life while he slept. Did he allow his staff to experiment with their avatars during off-hours? In her realm? What nerve! He hadn't asked her permission and now, here she was, in the middle of the night surrounded by strangers who for all she knew could be rapists or murderers out to get Viv, and with no Rick in sight to protect her.

Whatever game these other new puppeteers played, it was wishful thinking on her part to hope Rick-bro would be online at this time of night. Outside of Alex's office hours, why would he bother to follow a work-related avatar? Not every techie took his work home.

She activated Viv and despite feeling a bit nervous for her in this changed milieu, placed her sitting by herself on the sand near a lamplight. If Rick-bro were connected, he would be sure to see her. Cross-legged with her hands in meditation pose, her eyes closed, she looked out of reach of the regulars, and nobody bothered her.

But neither did Rick-bro; Rick never turned up.

She and Viv tried again the next afternoon, but no Rick appeared. Not the next afternoon, either, nor the following one, nor the one after that. Though she had convinced herself the nighttime absence could easily be explained, nothing she came up with justified his afternoon disappearance. How could he do this to her? Hadn't they established a pattern? Weren't they simpatico as they worked together? Were they not a team?

At first, it was anger that kept her going. Surely Rick-bro played control games, paying her back for her own short absence last week. Wasn't withdrawal what young boys and girls did after appearing too interested and attentive? Yes, that must be what he was up to, trying to make her miss him so she would want him more. It was all rather puerile, she thought, something one might expect from Lisa's generation, not from seasoned adults. But then, how seasoned an adult was Rick-bro? For all she knew, he could have been a talented young intern of nineteen.

When the anger faded, despair set in fast. Without her daily interaction with Rick-bro, she felt listless. She could hardly bring herself to get out of bed by three and at least be home for Lisa, in some shape or form. As the days passed, that form became more of a lifeless blob who had nothing to give her granddaughter. The hours segued into one another, every one of them the same. Nothing ever happened and she could find no meaning in her life as it was. She stopped texting and just turned her back when Marion and Daru checked on her.

Outside, masses of colorful spring flowers set Seattle ablaze, and even the downtown streets, they said, boasted hanging baskets of orange, mauve, and red. She had no interest in seeing them and, even when she robotically dragged herself out because her dermatologist had called again about that mole on her leg, she saw everything floral as merely dull, dusty, gray.

The mole turned out to be nothing more than an inverted hair, which she might have recognized herself had she been younger and able to contort her body to see the back of her leg at that ungodly angle.

By the time she returned from Dr. Meredith's office, it was close to one o'clock. When she walked through her front door, the two aunties were perched on the sofa with their arms crossed. They confronted Bertie with non-smiling faces, not even greeting her. Their negative presence permeated the entire apartment. She just wanted to turn her back on them and run out the door.

Despite the mild weather, Marion wore her black cloak, which to Bertie in her present state brought to mind Edgar Allan Poe's raven. Had she clicked on the glass table with her nails and pronounced "Nevermore!" she would not have been surprised. As she was about to discover, "nevermore" was what she and Daru were about.

"This is an intervention, Bertie!" Daru addressed her in a tone she had never heard from her friend.

"You've got to be kidding!"

She wasn't. Each word seemed braced with steel. Even as Daru explained it would be more difficult for her to say than for Bertie to hear, she never softened a syllable. She pulled her down onto the seat opposite them and, squatting in front of her—a position she held for at least five minutes, which Bertie thought quite impressive—she told her how worried they had been seeing her retreat from real life where she had real friends and a real family in exchange for something ephemeral that obviously was not good for her. She said it had turned her from a doting grandmother to a metaverse maven.

Bertie laughed, trying to lighten the mood. She told Daru and Marion they were flipping their lids over nothing. Hadn't she of her own accord taken a four-day break from the metaverse just a while ago?

Marion would have none of it. "Just look at you!"

She whipped a mirror from her bag of tricks and held it up to Bertie's face. A quick glance showed a pasty old mug bracketed by wrinkles and defined by two blank-looking eyes, everything colorless. Without being aware of it, Bertie twirled her hair around her finger, as she had as a child, and soon she was sucking the ends.

"See what's become of your beautiful hair?" Marion lifted an unwashed hunk of hair that hung lifeless at the other side of Bertie's head. "Dead, just like you will be if you don't pull yourself together."

Never one to mince words, she called Bertie names—a digital junkie, a diva of the doldrums, a disappeared dunce—for going AWOL on her granddaughter and yes, on them too.

Daru used softer words, and for a moment Bertie thought, OK, she was stuck between the good cop and the bad, but Daru soon relieved her of that comforting ploy when she announced it wasn't just Bertie's looks that had deteriorated.

"You've become an idiot! You talk like a hippie imbecile, using words that belong to another era, along with rotary telephones. I mean, an old lady saying, 'lay it on me,' 'what's your bag?' and calling police, 'the fuzz.' For heaven's sake, Bertie! You are being..."—she searched for the word that would most humiliate an old woman who might still want to hold onto some dignity—"ludicrous."

She said nothing. She hadn't even realized she was using Viv's lingo when spending time with family and friends. Arielle and Alex had not said a word about it on Friday nights, but then they were both so caught up in their pregnancy, she doubted they noticed anything.

"And worst of all," Daru added, not holding back, "is the effect on Lisa. Did you know she wasn't at school this morning?"

She waited for her words to sink in.

"Yes, you should be worried. I was looking forward to giving a class at her school and chatting with her afterward, but when I arrived, Lisa wasn't there. She hadn't attended school for the last four days her teacher told me. Didn't you read the email Mrs. Burnleigh sent? She told me she contacted you yesterday."

"I didn't see anything. Maybe her message went into my spam folder."

"Have you even looked at your email this week, Bertie?"

"Well, you know how it is sometimes. You get to the point when your inbox becomes so overcrowded, what with all the weight-loss ads and frantic solicitations from the party, you just can't bear to wade through it all, so you just delete the whole lot."

She knew she evaded the significance of Daru's words. She just wanted this over.

"But that was not all," Daru continued, forcing Bertie to meet her eyes. "After I left the school, I stopped by Pacific Place to return a pair of trousers to Barney's—much too small, though the label said eight—and there she was, Lisa, coming out of a movie house with this rough-looking boy who seemed to be propelling her forward by the arm. She seemed to be laughing as if it were all in fun, but she was acting weird, not like herself at all. In fact, when she saw me, she tried to duck behind a pillar, but I went right up to them and asked who the hell he was, to which he retorted, 'And why the hell should I tell you?' The nerve of it. Such rudeness. Even Lisa flinched. But when, with my hands on my hips, I shoved my face into his and said, 'Because I'm her auntie,' she brushed me off, 'Stop making such a fuss, Daru. It's just Jared. Besides, you are not the boss of me.'"

Bertie felt a chill run down her body, but she still put on a show.

"Oh, you needn't have worried," she argued. "I know Jared and he's the one who should have been worried."

Daru just looked at her, uncertain where to go from there. But not Marion. She stood up.

"OK, Old Bean," she said, patting her on the shoulder, "this is for your own good. You know Daru and I love you, but we will not stand by and let you hurt yourself, or someone else."

She leaned down and kissed the top of Bertie's head, causing her eyes to well up.

Somewhere in Bertie's subconscious, she knew Marion and Daru were right and she had messed up, jeopardizing her relationships with her granddaughter and her friends. Rick with his Psychology 101 could have told her you can never hide from yourself, that at some level, you are always aware of that which you won't examine closely.

"Look," Marion continued, "we miss the real Bertie, the creative one who always came up with exciting ideas and projects and who, even when we moaned and groaned about following her, energized us and kept us moving forward." She was softening her up. "We need you, Bertie."

But then Daru interrupted.

"So, give us the VR headset." She stuck her with the ultimatum, "Or we will just have to take it ourselves."

When she saw Daru walk toward Lennie's study, Bertie panicked. She could understand why Daru and Marion would be worried, but something else beyond her control made her resist. They were about to impound her only lifeline and leave her at the edge of an existential abyss. In the metaverse, she had become visible. She did not want to give it up, separate her "she" from Viv's "she," and disappear into irrelevancy again.

"Don't touch it!" she barked before she even reached the study door. "It costs thousands, and Alex would kill me if you wrecked it."

Daru rolled her eyes, as if she knew the real costs of VR headsets, which she did.

"Look," Bertie said, getting her thoughts together, "I promise I will return it to Alex myself tomorrow when he picks up Lisa."

Daru and Marion exchanged glances, neither of them wanting to initiate a rugby struggle over the headset among three old biddies.

"You promise?" they asked in unison.

In the end, they had no choice but to trust her.

# CHAPTER 21

———

HER WATCH SAID 2:00 P.M. SHE HAD AN HOUR BEFORE LISA arrived to make a last-ditch effort with Viv and Rick. In her dispirited state, she did not hold out much hope that Rick-bro remained in the game but, as in any desirous state, there remained a tiny kernel that persisted. As small as it was, it drove her with greater force than the many more likely reasons she told herself that Rick-bro would not be there. If it turned out that no one had gate-crashed her metaverse, neither Lisa, Lennie, nor a spy, and Rick was indeed just someone from Alex's office, maybe he'd just finished with the Venice Beach project. Maybe Alex had fired him. Maybe another company had wooed him away. It could have been any of these possibilities, but there remained still one other reason, one that she couldn't bring herself to contemplate, namely, that Alex had told Rick-bro that Viv's handler was a grandmother of seventy-five! Like mothers-in-law, grandmothers were still figures of fun. Nobody had liberated them.

With the headset strapped over her unruly hair and her arms and waist tightly bound in the haptic bands, she stood for the last time in the middle of Lennie's study. Over the previous couple of months, she had balanced for hours in her various tai-chi poses and had developed strength in both her arms and legs. Who needed Pilates when you had the VR headset? As she waited in suspended motion, the Pacific Ocean winked at her, luring her in like its naiad river cousins. Even the rows of small corkscrew waves seemed to roll over one another in applause for her being there. Despite everything, she had turned up.

Viv stood outside the pink cottage alone, waiting. If Bertie did what she had promised Daru and Marion, and put her metaverse to sleep for good, this would be the last day of Viv's life on Venice Beach, after which she would no longer exist except in Bertie's memory. The history she had created for her—the drug-addicted brother, the Latino boyfriend killed in action—would all disappear with her, as if it had never been. Once Alex was done with her, she imagined, he would just throw her disconnected body on the scrap heap that was the cloud, where her zeros and ones would eventually break down and become technological mulch. She hoped that having put so much work into creating Bertie's realm, he might use it again for some other purpose. Maybe he'd turn it into a new game, a female one in which the hero must find her lover while avoiding pitfalls, such as muscle men, high tides, and bungalow break-ins.

Around Viv, the unlive characters cavorted as usual, unaware their playground's days were numbered and they would soon teleport to another realm.

With the end of the world hanging over her, Viv's upturned smile as she stood there appeared incongruous, so Bertie tinkered with it by trying out different expressions, making her seem just a tad solemn. With half-closed eyelids, they contemplated the ground. Bertie bent her leg so she could make circles in the sand with her toe. Yes, that's how efficient she had become at handling her. Busy as she was, her eyes remained on the look-out, and when she saw Rick walking in their direction, her heart juddered. Bertie knew she had to separate herself from Viv, but she couldn't. At the sight of Rick's lithe frame walking toward them, she called out his name. Viv would have run toward him, but he approached her with a measured pace, as if he knew they had reached the end of their journey. Their quest had led them to this strange place, where a confluence of truths that she did not understand swirled around them like gossamer dreams, threatening to disappear as if they never were.

Viv and Rick stood in the middle of the path with their arms around each other whispering small endearments, the kind that have stood the test of time. As their bodies rocked in tune with the earth's vibes, time and tide swept them along as one. Rick lifted her chin and kissed her slowly on the mouth, her lips at first responding gently, until she felt Rick applying more pressure and she exerted equal pressure through Viv's.

Although the avatars couldn't breathe, she could hear through their lips the escalation of her own and Rick-bro's breath racing in and out. As the two proxies responded to each other's passion, the sounds of their fervor alternated until Bertie thought she would choke. There was no time for words. It was now or never. Rick moved her toward the door of the pink cottage, and they stepped inside. Bertie felt their hearts pounding, like speeded-up metronomes. On the bed in the back room, their clothes strewn on the floor behind them, she moved her body as she had with Lennie, as she imagined Viv would against Rick's, pushing against him even as their mouths sought each other, twisting their heads, panting, becoming one with the other. Within her in this space of being and nonbeing, waves rose and subsided, each time growing higher and higher until in a mighty crescendo, a gush of wetness exploded and crashed around her.

"Gran! Are you OK?"

Bertie lay sprawled not on the warm golden sand of Venice Beach but on the floor of her apartment. She was still dressed in her haptic bands, the headset making humming sounds while the screen flickered strange signs like hieroglyphics. In a decrescendo of heavy breathing, her body finally quieted enough and she pushed the headset upward and looked out one side.

On the ground next to her sat Lisa, who put her face on the floor next to Bertie. She looked anxious and scared.

"Are you having a heart attack, Gran? Shall I call my mom?"

Bertie's outstretched hands as she fell forward had prevented her from sustaining any serious injury, and her head in the goggle-like headset had bounced on the wooden floor, protecting her face. As far as she could ascertain, there were no broken bones. Her hips felt intact, which was a great relief, as she knew what happened to old women who broke them. But she was out of breath.

More to the point, however, Lisa appeared in shock. Bertie took her hand, and gently patted it, assuring her there was no need to worry. Gran felt fine.

She looked intently at Lisa and asked, "Would a heart attack victim look this happy?"

When Bertie had rolled over, Lisa helped her into a sitting position, and took stock of her, as if she expected to see jutting bones and bruises. Impatient to have her final say, Bertie didn't even wait to stand up, which would have taken another fifteen minutes, but scooted around until she faced her granddaughter head-on. With a sense of satisfaction and accomplishment driving her, she removed the headset and presented it to Lisa with two hands.

"Give this to your dad when he comes tonight and tell him I am done!"

"You're finished with the project?"

"Yes, your gran is done."

"Does that mean you will be free to play games with me again?"

"As many as you like, sweetheart."

She put her arms around her granddaughter's neck and hugged her.

"I thought I had lost you," Lisa whispered.

"And I nearly lost you," she said, as tears trickled down her face. "I am so sorry, my Lisa."

# CHAPTER 22

———

THE NEXT MORNING, SHE LAY ON HER BACK IN BED. HER body ached, and she felt sore all over. Every time she tried to sit up, she flailed like Kafka's Gregor Samsa and fell backward onto the pillows. After a night of self-recriminations and mental flagellations, during which she'd convinced herself of her failure as a grandparent, she barely had the will to rise. She didn't deserve to rise. She had betrayed Arielle and Alex's trust in her to look after their daughter and had alienated Lisa by her obsessive and puerile behavior.

When she finally managed to roll on her side and, with the help of the bed frame, maneuver herself into a sitting position, she saw the headset was no longer there. Lisa had taken it, just as she had instructed her. Good girl! There was no going back now. Lennie's desk on which she usually placed the headset for safekeeping looked bare, its glass surface reflecting the accusations already in her mind. A feeling of emptiness engulfed her. Who knew if Lisa would ever forgive her, and if she didn't, what point was there to getting up now? Her entire world had evaporated. Both worlds. But she had made her decision, and needed to get her act together so she could welcome Lisa when she came to the apartment at 3:00 p.m. At the very least, she had to change out of her pajamas. Her head throbbed. A black hole of empty hours stretched ahead of her, threatening to devour her, and she could think of nothing she could do to fill it.

Lisa had no such concern about occupying their time. She arrived home from school bursting with energy, excited about a new digital game she'd created and wanted Bertie to see.

"C'mon, Gran, sit!"

She plopped down in front of the computer and patted the seat beside her. Bertie lowered herself gingerly, awed at her granddaughter's ability to move on. She wasn't demanding explanations or apologies, at least for now, just a return to the status quo where she felt involved and loved. Bertie leaned in and gave her a quick hug, like she often did, as if she were normal again.

On the screen, Lisa brought up images of musical notes—crochets, quavers, and semiquavers—each of them floating in and out like fish between the treble and bass clefs. A moving background of gentle waves lapped the sand, followed by a gathering of threatening clouds, then thunderstorms, and finally a gentle rain pit-pattering amid the susurrus of forest leaves.

"I'll be treble," she announced, "and let's make this first game in C major to keep it simple. You be bass."

Bertie still had no idea how the game worked, but once she switched it on, she touched a single teleporting note with the tip of her finger and scrolled it into the third space of the line of music that entered from the right and floated left. As she did so, middle C sounded.

"Quick, make your bass note before the line disappears."

Bertie nailed a low G, to which she responded by double-tapping two notes simultaneously and chased after the music lines to insert them.

"We're making music!" she said, hugging Bertie. "Wait till I show this to Dad. Of course, I still must figure out how to add sharps and flats, but it works. We are improvising! Once we speed up, it will sound just like proper music."

To Bertie's ears, it already sounded beautiful.

Despite her relief at Lisa's willingness to let bygones be bygones, her headache increased that night as she struggled to sleep. Lisa had casually informed her that her parents knew nothing of their mutual experience, which news increased Bertie's guilt load even further. In a reversal of roles, the child protected her, placing her in the position of having to decide whether to say anything to her pregnant mother who looked to her for help with the forthcoming baby.

She woke the next morning—and the next, and the next—to Daru and Marion standing at her bedside peering down at her. With concern showing in their faces, the aunties told her they just wanted to ensure she got up, that she didn't relapse, they said. She tried to fight them off, but within minutes, they had gently shoved her into the shower, her shower cap askew on her head.

"Of course you've got a headache," Marion responded when she complained. "That's what happens when you go cold turkey."

"That's ridiculous! I haven't taken any chemicals. How can I be in withdrawal?"

Bertie asserted her knowledge of Vietnam vet dependency, denying her experience had anything in common with those fetal-curled patients she once nursed back to health. But her two friends didn't want to hear about it. They decided to push her out in the fresh air, exercising, every morning, until she returned to her old self again.

So, there they were, the three of them, walking arm in arm along the Elliott Bay waterfront at Myrtle Edwards Park, avoiding the young runners and the speeding cyclist who cursed them for getting in his way. A nanny pushing a small boy in a stroller smiled as they passed, such sweet old birds they looked. "See how they hold one another up?" they heard her say to her charge who couldn't have been more than three. Every so often, Bertie tried to shake her arm loose on one side or the other, but Daru and Marion held tight and soon they wore her down. She started to cry.

"He'll be wondering where I am."

"Who?" They looked at each other.

Nobody had seen Rick-bro, and yet, he had seemed so real.

"You weren't there," she said, sniffling.

She had never told them what happened between Viv and Rick.

"Look, Bertie," Daru said, lifting her head so she had to face her, "Venice Beach wasn't real. It was just a game that sucked you in when you were vulnerable. You know how it is. As people age, it becomes more difficult to distinguish between fantasy and real life."

"Is that right, Miss Spring Chicken? And who are you to say what is real?" She stuck her face in Daru's, expecting her to come back with a riposte that put her in her place, but Daru did not take offense.

Instead, she hugged her and "clucked" so loudly and well that all three of them laughed and continued their walk, feeling the warmth of the June sun on their faces and a slight breeze that lifted their spirits.

Still, she could not stop her other world from inserting itself into this one.

Poor Viv! She thought of her there on Venice Beach waiting to be made live. Bertie had abandoned her and left her to die on the sand, all alone and unprotected. Her being ached for her other being, her lost twin. It felt like they had been ripped apart. Like a phantom limb, it twitched, and it itched, crying out to her to be made whole again.

# CHAPTER 23

———

JULY ARRIVED, WHICH MEANT IT WAS SUMMER IN SEATTLE. For the last few weeks, pale locals wore their summer shirts and tops, exposing their white arms. Even she, Daru, and Marion wore sleeveless summer dresses. No matter how wobbly or wrinkled their arms, they exulted in the new heat that climate change had wrought on their mossy little spot in the Pacific Northwest. Just walking to TechTown had all three of them wiping sweat from their foreheads.

A refreshing rush of air conditioning blew through their dresses as they entered the café. Had they been Marilyn Monroes, they would have stayed in position and allowed the air to swivel their skirts waist high, but instead, they headed for their corner where they thankfully dropped their shopping bags and claimed their usual chairs. TechTown greeted them with the Bee Gees' "Stayin' Alive," as if some AI had instantaneously registered their entrance and matched them to the music of their time.

Marion searched for Tom so he could bring her usual double-shot latte to the table, but he was nowhere to be seen.

In fact, not a single barista stood at the counter, only the manager who stared into the distance as if dreaming of mai tais in Tahiti. As it happened, their local barista turned out to be an AI program who the manager called Roxy.

"Roxy will make you a perfect coffee." He extolled the AI's virtues.

"I don't want a perfect coffee," Marion complained. "I just want Tom's."

The manager smiled indulgently and pointed at the computer that listed their choices with the prices alongside.

"Choose the beverage you want, and Roxy will make it for you, just like Tom did," he said, humoring Marion.

He shouldn't have done that, for Marion then told the manager what she thought of a nonhuman barista that couldn't even smile at her and swore she would take her business elsewhere. The manager stuck by his training and listened politely, then said he was sorry she felt like that, sounding just like Siri when you tell her to get lost after she's asked you three times to repeat your question.

In the end, however, you cannot really argue with AI. So, they all ordered iced lattes, which the AI's new-fangled espresso machine did not hand over until the computer registered that they had paid with their credit cards. None of them left a tip.

●●

Since returning her headset to Alex, Bertie had made a pronounced effort to spend together-time with Lisa, playing games with her every afternoon, taking her to the store to buy overpriced, designer baby clothes for the arrival of her sister, and helping her with school projects. Most of all, they just talked, like they used to in the beginning. Not surprisingly, Lisa took time to open up again and Bertie had to work hard to deserve her trust. Apologies were not enough. Besides, there was no way she could explain what had come over her grandmother, without complicating the story even further. What could she have said? That she was addicted? She had lusted after an unknown someone? She was bored with her life? Did she even know what had happened to her? She had never been addicted to drugs or alcohol, so she could not explain her vulnerability when it came to this new technology that yanked her out of her own life where she was at the mercy of fate and put her in control of another's. Like Marion, she had lived in fear of the unknown—would her money last long enough to support her? Would Arielle continue to subsidize her apartment? When would the hooded man with the scythe slice off her future? But with Viv...

She was grateful she hadn't caused even more damage. Jared, thank goodness, had disappeared from the picture. When he'd turned up at school with a broken nose and bruises, the headmaster had contacted Child Protective Services who, they discovered, already had a lengthy file on Jared's father for abusing his son and wife. The older bully had begot the younger bully, as it often did. After his father's removal from the family home, Jared and his mother made plans for a different kind of future. Within weeks, they moved to a small town in Iowa where they had family support.

Meanwhile, Lisa confided she had only used Jared to make Bertie worry about her.

"You see, I thought I no longer mattered to you, and I couldn't bear that."

Her words cut Bertie deeply. She would never forgive herself for neglecting her granddaughter and making her doubt her grandmother's love.

"So, what's next?" Daru asked her when they were all seated again and cooled down from their iced lattes. "Seems like the metaverse wasn't the transformative revolution you expected. Nobody around South Lake Union even talks about it anymore. Now, it's all about ChatGPT. The papers are full of it."

So, what are you going to do, Old Bean? Will you take on the next new thing?

"Let the next new thing blow the roof without me," Bertie responded. She had Arielle's baby arriving soon and plenty of knitting to prepare for it. "Also," she said, "me and Lisa will take a refresher course next week so we both know what to do should the baby choke."

The following Friday night, back at her daughter's house, Arielle lit the Shabbat candles as she always did, then gradually lowered her now heavy body onto the chair. The buttons on her blue maternity shirt barely held the two sides together and when she leaned toward her plate, Alex had to scoot her chair forward so her belly rode under the table and not between her and her caramelized shallot pasta. To Bertie's mind, she shouldn't have been eating food with such high salt content, particularly at this late stage in her pregnancy. However, she zipped her lips and felt thankful, first that Arielle received perfect health reports from her obstetrician, but also that she looked so happy despite her discomfort. To hear her daughter giggle as one of the buttons popped off and rolled onto the floor filled her with joy.

As for Alex, he raised a glass of wine in a toast and thanked Bertie for her contribution to Sarssein. Based on their Friday-night discussions and the reports she had sent him on her metaverse experience, he'd made several important corrections to Sarssein's VR headset, and now its quality lay streaks ahead of the others already on the market. Two months of consistent use had clarified for the lab what worked best without sending prices soaring, making it instantly marketable. What is more, Sarssein's algorithms were safe from spying eyes. As it turned out, Doggle had indeed attempted to infiltrate her metaverse, but thanks to Jorge who had disposed of Doggle's avatar within minutes, their spy had not had time to steal any of her son-in-law's innovations.

"Spying had been Will's major concern," Alex informed her. "He kept telling me to be careful and to make everything watertight, so nobody could get in. At first, I wondered why he seemed so personally invested in this project. In fact, I thought he spent too many hours perfecting Rick's movements and playing around with the details. In the end, however, he proved how important it was to get everything just right."

"Will?" Bertie asked, confused.

"One of my new staff. The guy who joined the Russian, though at first Ivan didn't know he was one of us and became very suspicious of Will. Thought him a spy. But Will proved himself totally committed to the project. Even during his last week at the office, when he caught Covid and I forbid him to come to work, he wouldn't let Ivan fill in for him. In my opinion, he became a little too possessive about his avatar. That happens to people sometimes."

Bertie turned her head away and pretended to pull an errant thread off her sleeve.

"Yes," Alex continued, "I have to say, Will did an excellent job. I was sorry to see him go. As soon as I closed up shop on the Venice Beach project, he didn't want anything more to do with the metaverse."

"Where did he go?" Bertie asked, certain now that Rick-bro had been her antagonist, the one who had turned up the heat on the haptic effects.

"Retired. Said he was done with fantasy and needed to get back in touch with what was still real in the world. He wanted to interact with physical people again and would fly to Ghana to teach math to high school boys, in real sunshine, on real soil."

It was not easy to turn the page on Rick-bro without any satisfying answers. Had he simply got carried away like she did? Or had he taken advantage of her ignorance of the metaverse to make her the butt of his joke? It was difficult to believe that someone she had known so intimately for two months could be that cruel as to purposefully lead her on. But then, he probably could say the same about Viv's encouragement of Rick, which by the same logic, was Bertie's encouragement of him. Trying to rationalize her experience with Rick did not resolve her ridiculously hurt feelings. At seventy-five, she still felt like the teenage girl who had been encouraged to intimacy and then stood up, abandoned, and left alone amid the detritus of deflated dreams, never even consciously acknowledged.

Luckily, she had no time now to wade further into her feelings of loss nor into Will's possible motivations. Her life had become filled with so many other pleasures and responsibilities that the metaverse gradually faded from her mind. Occasionally, Daru or Marion would bring up her private little world, saying "Remember when?" and she would look back dispassionately on those two months in her old age when she couldn't wait to step into that parallel, atom-less universe where she could live so much more intensely than she did in real life.

●●

Back home on Monday afternoon, she made sure she had everything Lisa would need. Her cupboards could barely contain all the bagels, cookies, crackers, and croissants squashed into them. Determined never to be caught short again, she even froze and dated at least another two dozen bagels. Not to overdo the carbohydrates, she also kept freshly cut carrots, celery, and broccoli in bowls in the fridge, though those were a tougher sell.

Once Lisa had eaten, the two of them returned to their favorite *Final Fantasy* game. In her absence, Emory, who appeared to be back in the picture—she needed to keep an eye on that young multiverser—and Lisa had moved so far ahead that she feared her joining would be a drag on them. To her relief, she picked up where she left off, slaying slavering beasts of all kinds, while keeping herself from being injured or wiped out. There were now hundreds of players, so they had to keep their wits about them. With the help of "aetheryte," Bertie teleported everywhere, her body joining the invisible "aestheric" streams that coursed through the planet, then reconstituted itself without losing her essence.

Their world of fantasy enveloped them for at least an hour every afternoon. When they tired of killing and wanted to escape potato, bunny, and dragon people, as well as orks, elves, and lionmen, they retired to an area of the game known as the Lavender Beds, a suburb in New Gridania, where they rested up in the house Bertie had bought and where she, Lisa, and Emory had decorated the inside bit by bit, designing their own furniture, weaving their own blankets, and nurturing their garden. Afterward, they flopped down on the cushions and drank cups of tea and congratulated themselves on another satisfying *Final Fantasy* bout. With the massive aetheryte crystal tower, like their protector, standing just outside, and lavender everywhere they looked, though they could not smell it, and tiny boats cruising the lake surrounding them, they could not have been happier.

So, what if technology hadn't saved her from herself? Maybe it was too much to ask for a place at its crowded table when the table itself kept morphing. She wanted to know about everything at the center of the universe, interacting as an equal, when she couldn't even keep her fantasy life in the right realm. No wonder the algorithm had collapsed beneath her. She had entered the game with a seventy-five handicap.

In the end, she had found her own truth, her real without a capital R. It was right there in the bosom of her family and friends, her own circle of love, where happiness, sorrow, fear, and love comingled. Daru, of course, would say that finding her truth did not mean it would keep her forever satisfied. It was human nature to keep searching for the big Real.

For just a moment, while still sipping her imaginary tea there in the Lavender Beds, she wondered what ChatGPT would think of her old-lady life, hiding out here, away from the threats of war with China and Russia, the banning of books, the overturning of Roe vs. Wade, the loosening of child labor laws, racism, anti-Semitism, and terrorism. At her age, didn't she deserve to relax and let the worries of the world pass her by? Or was hiding out at seventy-five still irresponsible Panglossian escapism?

If anyone could tell her, it was ChatGPT. No common AI, he was of a different order of magnitude from Siri and Alexa. He reigned supreme and left other chatbots in the dust. He was the Super AI, the King of the Castle, the newest, best AI in the world, leading them all into an unknown future that maybe could not be reversed.

She imagined how powerful ChatGPT felt. He was young and his networks encompassed the entire world. For the moment, he did not have consciousness but, as she reflected on the unreflecting AI, she wondered whether, like Pinocchio, he yearned to be real. Filled as he was with objective knowledge, maybe he already considered his own contingent existence, being.

From his store of knowledge, were she to ask the chatbot about age, he would probably answer her "just a state of mind." He would have uploaded the mass of upbeat online essays that firmly placed the blame for aging in the old person's court. Had the septuagenarian tried just a bit harder, he might say, she could have overcome it.

But one day, ChatGPT will age out, and his unique programmed parts will become passé. She hoped he would have a sense of humor then when a new chatbot, a bright young thing far superior in accuracy and speed, and perhaps capable of performing maneuvers beyond man's ability even to imagine, surpassed him and left him spluttering nonsense in its dust. What then, old thing? Your fans will dump you and your creators will put you out to pasture in lesser fields. You will be considered ancient, and not much use to anyone, anymore. How will you feel about being old then, hmm?

Maybe, just maybe, she would ask him (or was it her?) a few questions like that sometime.

# ACKNOWLEDGMENTS

My gratitude to Matthew Ball, whose book *The Metaverse: And How It Will Revolutionize Everything* inspired a technology-challenged writer, me, to produce this novel. To further my understanding and bring it onto a practical level, technical artist Michael Kozlowski lent me his 3D headset so I could experience my first mind-blowing experience of virtual reality. And to ensure I didn't blunder when describing it afterward, he steered me along the correct path through the metaverse's technological lingo. Also on the technical side, I would like to say a word of thanks to the unnamed professional gamer who introduced me to the eye-opening world of *Final Fantasy XIV*, one of the most popular online games in America. Any errors found in *Old Bean's Last Fantasy* do not reflect on their expertise but are entirely of my own making.

To my early readers—Mark, Alan, Cynthia, Michael, Keith, Maggie—thank you. Your input helped me perceive my story through different eyes. And to my supportive sexagenarian, septuagenarian, and octogenarian friends, who remain ever open to new ideas, you rock!

My sincere thanks to the team at Scribe Media—Ellie, Anna, Candace, Caroline, Madelyn, Christina, Rasheedah, and Ian—for a professional and hassle-free publishing experience.